The Music of Madness

The Music of Madness

Tracy L. Harris

Writers Club Press
San Jose New York Lincoln Shanghai

The Music of Madness

All Rights Reserved © 2001 by Tracy Lynn Harris

No part of this book may be reproduced or transmitted in any form or by any means, graphic, electronic, or mechanical, including photocopying, recording, taping, or by any information storage retrieval system, without the permission in writing from the publisher.

Writers Club Press
an imprint of iUniverse, Inc.

For information address:
iUniverse, Inc.
5220 S. 16th St., Suite 200
Lincoln, NE 68512
www.iuniverse.com

ISBN: 0-595-21256-5

Printed in the United States of America

For my family,
Norman, Sandra, Todd, Wendy, Tom, Svetlana, and Ellen
the personification of unconditional love.

Truth

I walk slowly,
in the deep grass.
Feeling its long–fingered blades
softly touch me,
caressing the bareness of my legs as I walk through the night.

It's cold and the sky is black,
and the sky is moonless in its blackness,
but punctured with the light of stars.

I lay down in the beckoning
deepness of the grass,
longing for its comfort and warmth,
and see
the countless stars,
so clear
that I reach out to touch them, but I can't.
I sense that there is more to see and feel than my mind can capture.
The thought chills me and I try to pull the long grasses around me.
Is this the truth or is this my truth alone?
Or is it that part of the night that fills my soul with questions?
Does the doe, moving quickly by,
know how to touch the stars?
Or, unlike the doe, must I wait for life's dark ending
to lift my soul to the heavens and finally touch the truth?

Tracy L. Harris

Contents

Foreword xi
Preface xv
Prologue: The Tarantella 1

Chapter 1   The Refrain of Youth 7
         Reverberations of Happiness

Chapter 2   The Refrain of Love's Lost 27
         Overtures to Anguish

Chapter 3   The Angry Soprano 57
         The Dissonant Opera of my Psychosis

Chapter 4   A Mind's Crazy Cadenza 87
         Messages from An Alternate Reality

Chapter 5   My Life's Ultimate Dissonance 109
         Suicide and the Asylum

Chapter 6   Recovering My Mind's Inner Harmony . . . 151
         Quieting The Discord Within

Chapter 7   A Sweet Series of Encores 175
         Winning the War

Epilogue: A Complete Individual Despite a Brain Disorder . . 189

Foreword

The Music of Madness stands alone as a landmark text; a true exploration of the human mind gone awry. It does not wear the social masks of our typical interactions; it does not carry the behavioral screens, which hide the inner tortures that can occur in a mind which is in conflict with itself. This exploration of the human mind, delves directly into the inner workings of our mind/brain as it becomes distorted with illness. *The Music of Madness* takes you directly into Ms. Harris' mental world so that you can experience along with her, her altered stream of consciousness, the horrifying delusions and the extreme depression. This pioneering book gives you, for the first time, an intimate, direct view of a mind in disarray as though you were living it yourself.

Read this book with the understanding that it is a window on the mind/brain in action, tormented by a growing distortion of reality. This book thus creates an experience almost like watching a brain surgeon, showing to his gallery the functions of the patient's brain, by opening the skull and its protective coverings and inserting electric probes into various parts of that exposed, fragile organ, to reveal the diseased parts. Through *The Music of Madness*, you are privileged to see the workings of important brain dysfunctions first hand and feel the pain of a mental disorder alongside the author, as she experiences it.

This author's exploration of her disease from a primarily stream–of–consciousness viewpoint, gives us an affecting and very direct picture of the mental torments that literally change her cognitive capabilities and destroy her ability to perform her beloved music by distorting it and causing her to see, think, plan and take actions that are aberrant and irrational.

This book describes the live mind/brain, fighting within itself in a literal death struggle for control of one individual's actions and destiny, thus making this autobiographical case study unique among books on mental illness.

The author made a brave choice in giving us an unadorned picture of her mind/brain in transition, which only an individual who has experienced such a mental disorder could accurately describe. We see the innermost parts of the author's brain in a fight for control over her life itself. It is this very intimate fight to retain her sanity that the author describes vividly in telling the story of her fight to achieve some degree of normalcy and humanness once again.

This book is the first real insight of the inner workings of the mind/brain, written in simple straightforward language, described by the best person available, the victim; the person who lived with Schizoaffective Disorder and survived it to once again gain control of her mind and body and write about it.

Those of us who have been fortunate enough to possess a normal brain, see reality as we were meant to see it; colorful, dynamic and direct. Normal reality consists of three levels of perception and understanding, but the diseased brain introduces a fourth reality, which is like a nightmare that has come to life. This fourth reality is not formed from true meaning and the attachment of knowledge learned, but is invented for its own purposes out of a chaotic mixture of experience, environmental exposure and the myriad memories that have been accumulated, all within a sick mind. This fourth reality is what makes mental illness so disruptive. The mentally ill reach for what reality they have and often times, find it missing, or distorted, or frightening and they do not know how to function within this bizarre world.

This fourth reality does not destroy intelligence, it does not destroy the ability to feel and respond, it just means that the mentally ill must fight even harder to separate their view of the world through those smoky, transparent panes of glass, into a vision within which they can fight and survive, dream, love and discover, as other people do.

Tracy Harris gives us the full breadth of this devastating disease in living color, creating a mosaic of moods, feelings and emotions contained within a brain fighting against itself. Her text is shocking, revealing and intensely personal. We can all leave this book with a better understanding of the human condition, ourselves and the silent suffering that is mental illness.

The Pacific Center for Advanced Studies

Preface

Originally, this book began as a therapeutic exercise, a personal work written just for me. Many nights, when I tired of practicing my flute and found myself still unable to sleep, I would sit down at my computer and write about my life, my loves, my music, my triumphs, my losses and ultimately the many things that I have to be thankful for. As the number of pages in this very personal work increased, I began to ask myself; could one convey in mere words the horrendous experience of a brain disorder? I resolved to find out by turning my personal writings into a book, which places you, the reader, directly into my mind where you can think my thoughts alongside me, live through hallucinations with me, step inside my train of thought throughout the progression of my illness and experience, for yourself, the devastating effects of mental illness.

I spent a long time thinking about the repercussions of writing this book. What would people think of me once my "secret" was out? How would people treat me after I shared with the world the confusing insanity I have endured? Up until now I have shared my suffering with only my immediate family.

The diagnosis of schizoaffective disorder, for me, was long in coming. Until I received the right diagnosis I suffered from panic attacks, the crushing dissonance of depression, the weird, magnificent off-tuning of mania, terrifying hallucinations, suicide attempts, self-mutilation and a long bout with an eating disorder, all without appropriate medical help. I suffered a very long time from the results of one misdiagnosis after another, and it wasn't until my family began research in earnest, searching for and successfully finding a highly skilled psychopharmacologist, that I was able to begin my long recovery. This talented psychiatrist put a name to the often complicated, confusing, and ugly face of this disorder. I found that with his help and the use of proper medication, I could survive and even overcome the dysfunctions associated with my mental illness and go on to lead my life as it was meant to be.

Contained within the following pages are the highlights of my life and the depths of my despair so that you may understand the evolution of my mental disease and the pains and triumphs associated with surviving it. I want all of you to know that recovery is possible, that there is hope for a happy and productive life despite mental illness.

Acknowledgements

The magnificent journey from the whisper of a concept to a completed book cannot be achieved without the help of many wonderful people. I am very fortunate to have been surrounded by exceptionally intelligent, talented, accomplished and dedicated individuals. I wish to thank first and foremost Norman Harris, my father, who's enthusiastic support was invaluable to me during the preparation of this book and provided me with inspirational critiques and advice, without him this book would never have been completed. I also owe a great debt to my mother Sandra Harris who tirelessly honed and edited the countless versions of this book that I threw at her month after month and provided insightful and supportive comments throughout the entire process; without her love I would not be here today. I also would like to thank Ellen Hill, the matriarch of our family, for her love and support. I owe an immeasurable debt of gratitude to my brother Todd Harris, who despite being devastatingly ill and in incredible pain from kidney disease, continued to assist me in every way he could by supporting, encouraging, and loving me no matter how he was feeling. I would also like to thank his wife, my piano accompanist, Svetlana Rudikova for her unswerving optimism and perennial smile. I would also like to thank Wendy LeBlanc, my loving sister, talented concert harpist and performance partner for her incredible support throughout my entire illness and who has seen me at my worst yet loved me anyway. Special thanks also go to Tom LeBlanc for his tireless support of our entire family, warm encouragement and love. I would also like to thank my little nephew Robert Leblanc for his incredible ability to make me smile at myself and not take life so seriously.

I also would like to acknowledge the incredible support and encouragement I received from Dr. Robert H. Gerner who kept me grounded during some of the worst times in my life and brought me back from the brink on numerous occasions by allowing me to express myself through the written word. I also wish to thank Dr. Richard Danson who gave me invaluable advice about the book and not only supported me, but my family, when it was going through an extremely difficult time. I also would like to thank my literary agent Jodie Rhodes who has through this long process become an honorary member of my family. Her enthusiasm for and dedication to seeing this book in print has been second to none and I am so very thankful for all of her advice and support.

I am enduringly grateful to every one of you.

Prologue: The Tarantella

Come dance with me

In Taranto in the South of Italy a form of hysteria appeared around the 16th century involving the bites of tarantulas. It was said that victims of the bite of the poisonous tarantula spider could be cured by taking part in a frenzied dance, which was supposed to free the victim from the terrible consequences of being bitten. This dance had a rapid meter during which the victim turned more and more frantically to free herself of the spider's horrible venom. This special dance came to be known as the Tarantella.

I have been pacing the cold floor of my bedroom for hours. It is already 2:00 in the morning but I cannot sleep. I am afraid to sleep. I am afraid of what will happen when I shut my eyes. I stare with longing at my bed. My eyes are burning with fatigue, and my body speaks its silent language begging me for sleep. I hesitate once more at my bed and then listen for even the faintest noise within my room. I take a deep breath and hold it, trying to be as quiet as possible, but I hear only the rhythmic beat of my heart and the soft persistent ticking of the clock next to my bed. I try to move my mind from where it is, buried in the fear of this moment, to my last concert. I try to concentrate. What was my last concert? What did I play? Did I like the music? I cannot think. I only can listen for that dreaded sound. I try to think again of something else: I know who I am; at least I used to know who I am. I am a concert flutist. I think I am a good concert flutist and I am old enough at twenty–four years of age not to be afraid of the dark anymore. I remember those days when I was a young girl of five years and felt the unknown fear of the darkness, but I can't be hurt by the dark, even though my mind seems to keep saying to me that I can.

Now it is 3:30am and I feel no longer able to keep this awkward vigil. I am exhausted. I drop to my bed and quickly pull up the sheets and electric blanket around my neck, along with the rest of the blankets on my bed; struggling to make these silent guardians into an impenetrable my fortress. The blackness seems to intrude on my fortress world and I pull the blankets more tightly over my head. And there–there was something. Some tiny sound. My mind is now racing in desperate blinding panic. I am alone. I never wish to be alone, but I am alone. My parents, who could possibly save me, are miles away at the other end of the darkness. My door is closed; isolating me even more. I start to scream out but the sound is choked in my throat. I hear an even stronger sound. It seems to be coming from one of the walls. I can hardly breath. I feel as though my bed is at the top of a very, very narrow hill and in the dark I cannot seem to see an escape route. The hollow scratching sounds increase. I stop again and listen very hard. The sounds are now coming from several places within the wall. How can that be? The hollow space in the walls is too small for an animal. My mind races, trying to visualize what it could be, or what they could be, because now the sounds are coming from the ceiling as well as the walls. I want to race to the door, but in the blackness it is forever far away. It is beyond my reach. I feel weak. I am not sure that if I tried to stand up that I could. I cannot see the walls, but the persistent scratching tells me where they are, and they feel as though they are coming ever closer to my bed.

All I can do now is lie frozen underneath the blankets. I curl up in a tight ball, wishing I were back, secure in my mother's warm arms. How my heart is aching for the presence of anyone to hold me and tell me that it will be all right. With my knees practically touching my chin, I struggle down even farther under my protective blankets. The air becomes very close, pushing me with persistence to remove the blankets, but I know I can't do that or all will be lost. I can feel the moist breath, my own breath, on my hand. I know I will have to come out from under the covers and I feel faint with the dread of what I will find.

The scratching is much louder now. And I hear it from the walls, and the ceiling, with such intensity that it covers the sound of my frantic breathing, it covers the sound of my pounding heart, it covers the sound of the crickets outside my window. It becomes the only sound in my dark world. I struggle not to cry. I dare not give away my position. I don't know exactly what's coming, but I feel a deeper fear than any I have felt before. If I am to face death, this must be the noise with which it enters my room.

Sweat is dripping down the back of my neck and beading on my back. The heat under the blankets is stifling. My legs ache with the need to run. I dare not move. Now the noises tell me that what I dread is coming forth into my world. The sounds of the plaster being scraped away now send clear signals of bits of plaster falling onto the floor of my room. There is the unmistakable sound of the walls and ceiling breaking apart. I feel a deep shudder that I cannot seem to overcome. I recognize the unmistakable sound of spiders' legs scratching at the plaster. My heart is pounding so fast, that it is difficult now to catch my breath, as I force myself to turn on the light next to my bed. In the flash of light, even before my eyes become accustomed to the brightness, I see gaping holes all over the walls and a corner of the ceiling. I see long black hairy legs, which clearly belong to spiders feeling around outside the holes, with those sharp stuttering movements that only a spider can make.

The first spider enters my room through one of the holes. I can now see it clearly; it is a Black Widow with a body at least a foot long, a large black shiny ebony ball with legs. As it moves to leave the hole, others are trying to squeeze through, sometimes two or three at a time. As I look in horror, there are more of the same black spiders coming out from every hole. My walls look like some kind of surrealistic cheese, with spiders moving out of the holes and coming towards me.

They cover my gray carpet, until it takes on the blackness of their writhing bodies. Alive with their threatening movements. These monstrous spiders bear their large fangs, and venom drips from them, as they scan the room with their innumerable eyes; a sea of eyes staring at their prey. I can see, as I look at them in horror, my face distorted as it reflects from each unblinking, shining eye. I feel a numbness coming over my body. My mind races. I am horrified and fascinated simultaneously. Is this how God wants me to die? I yearn to faint, in hopes that in fainting I can be free of this tortured scene.

As I stare, with the belief of a victim facing her executioner, I can hear their legs scraping against the book covers in my bookcase and over the papers I have left on the floor. I can hear the sharp, crackle of their long prickly black legs as they catch in the fibers of my bedroom carpet. I can hear them in the ceiling, crawling over each other like a persistent army; each soldier trying to be the first to kill its victim.

As I watch in disbelief, I feel the sickening thud of one of these giants on my pillow, inches from my face. As I struggle to move, I thrash at this dark sentinel, trying to throw it from my bed. Oh God, if this is real, please take them away. Another one of them appears now at the foot of my bed. I think it is going to bite me. I throw the covers back now in total panic, and cold air forces me into a sickening alertness to my exposure. I lift my head away from the pillow as fast as I can; my pounding heart is now in my throat and I struggle to breathe, even though I am out from under my suffocating cocoon of blankets. I feel dizzy as I try to get up. My arms are tingling and my legs feel heavy with the weight of my fear.

I can see clearly now, in front of my clock face, the outline of another of these spiders that has landed where my head had just been on the pillow. The pillow sinks slowly under her weight. She is even larger than the others and by her rapid short movements; I can tell she is lightening fast. I can now see on this largest of the spiders, the distinctive bright red hourglass that means the kiss of death.

These Black Widows are now scurrying awkwardly toward me, bumping against each other in an effort to come straight to my body. The reality of this moment begins to sink into my mind, and coats all of my consciousness with the color of this horrible truth. They intend to bite me, one by one, until I am paralyzed and then wrap me in their sticky, tenuous webbing until I cannot move. They will then continue to bite me, while I am still alive, feeling the burning sting of each vicious bite. Feeling the life painfully draining my consciousness to the very end, until death grabs me from the warmth of the life I have, and drops me into the cold silent abyss of unfeeling eternity.

I look around my room quickly, before I move and see the horrible rubble these monsters have created. There is plaster dust everywhere, turning some of these black beings into white devils. I finally can take a deep breath and use its shocking energy to charge for the door. I must outrun them, but they are everywhere.

As I move toward the door, I feel them dropping on my body; on my hair, on my shoulders, on my back, on my legs, on my arms. Their weight is almost more than I can stand; I feel their legs scratching at my neck, the same legs that had scratched holes in the plaster walls. I madly swipe at my head and my back, desperately trying to knock them off and crush them. I succeed with a few, but others take their place. The floor is a sea of black legs, abdomens and eyes. I crush their sickening soft bodies under my feet, as I continue to move towards the door. I can feel their fangs scratching across the bare skin of my legs, as they try to pierce through my skin and inject their slimy toxin. My ears are ringing, as I finally reach the doorknob, twist it frantically and pull open the door. I slam the door quickly behind me. I can hear them flinging their bodies against the door and I see the door vibrate with their persistent impacts. I can see their long, black, shiny legs underneath the door, unrelenting, blindly feeling for their chosen victim. For me.

I run into my bathroom, turning on the light and locking the door behind me. I am almost afraid to look in my mirror to see if they have reached this room also. I look at my face, and see spiders clinging to my hair. I slap at my head with all my might, in an attempt to kill the last few. When I look back at the bathroom mirror, I see only the dimly lit walls. The spiders are gone. They have disappeared.

1

The Refrain of Youth

Reverberations of Happiness

I awaken slowly to that kind of odd antiseptic smell that only hospitals have. The sounds of the dreaded Tarantella still echo in my mind, but their content has the faintness of music reverberating against the concert wall. During my struggle with the vicious spiders I danced in ever–tighter circles, forcing my legs to move ever faster to rid the venom from my body, but the frenzied dance did not do its work. I remember falling to the floor and crying for help from my bathroom.

I realize now that my parents have taken me to a mental institution. At twenty–four years of age, I have lost this great battle one more time and I need the convalescence of a soldier who is shocked to the core of his soul from the horrors that he has witnessed. I am ready for the white sheets of the hospital and the comfort that a soldier deserves after such a battle. I feel I must sleep and my mind, with grace and sympathy, pulls a curtain across my eyes and all goes black. When I awaken, I can hear a quiet sob coming from the next room. They have taken my shoelaces, my belt, anything that might be a means of destroying my life. My life. The words seem empty, devoid of meaning, like an empty crate with sides rotting in the sun. My soul belongs to no one. I grieve for my music. I grieve for the love I have lost. My mind has lost its emotional ground; partly because my body no longer feels those experiences that life should give us. My brain is searching for that quiet place in a high, dry tree, where it can settle and watch the flood of debris and the human struggle that we call life, hoping to make some sense out of the fast stream of uncoordinated, chaotic, complex, desperate, painful information passing by its useless sensors. I slowly climb out of bed, sliding against the cold wall of the dark room, and feel the wall push dispassionately back against me as I seek its comforting stability. I wonder, as I feel the cold penetrate my back, if this mindless structure can give me comfort. I need the warmth of human touch but I am left with a concrete floor and a cold wall to remind me of the loneliness I feel at this moment.

I take a deep sigh and re–look at this room while idly fiddling with one big toe. How long does it take my brain to feel my big toe as I wiggle it with my little finger? I know I am wiggling it, I know that I can feel that I am wiggling it, but how long does it take for my poor tired neurons to tell me that vastly important message in this quiet solitude? Does it take a day? Does it take a millisecond? Is my mental space fractilized to where I cannot keep track of the detail? I am not sad about wiggling my toe, but I am not happy about it either, and will that get me closer to finding an answer to getting out of this damned room? Can I think about Berlioz and Brahms, Madame Curie and her x–rays, or William James getting out of bed on a cold morning and still feel my toe wiggling? If so, my mind's clearly capable of generating many thoughts. Are these thoughts reality? I used to think so. But how can those spiders, how can those dreaded moments fill my consciousness when I am so capable of thinking about so many other things? In fact, I know that our brain is more like a theater giving us a chance to see and feel our experiences in a way that lets information about our enemies and life and chance moments come together, so that we can make serious and reasoned choices about future actions. Some people have called this Will. Some people say Will can be free. Others argue that there are so many influences on your life and so many constraints from your culture that free Will cannot exist under such conditions. Whether it is free or not, I still feel that I have some Will left. Well, surely if I have enough Will left to wiggle my toe when I want to, I should be able to fight off the horrible delusions that fill my reality. I shift against the wall as I think these thoughts; I feel its coldness penetrating even more, reminding me that I still have some real feelings. At least I can still feel cold. I can't seem to feel love but I can still feel cold. So how long does it take for my brain to feel my finger wiggling my big toe? You know, come to think about it, I don't know if time even matters inside my mind. Neurons don't use clocks, neurons can't tell time. Time is a complicated thing, probably too complicated for me to fully understand now. Answer this question if you can: it's a cloudy day and you can see the clouds billowing in the sky, ever higher, as though to prepare for a storm in summer. The clouds represent a complexity of shapes, which come and go with a randomness that is hard to follow. If you look ever harder at the details of these clouds as they evolve and separate; dissolve and are reborn; is time moving forward while they do this? Or backward? If I were to take a motion picture of a small part of the sky, being careful to not let you see where the sun is or anything else other than the mass of moving clouds and I run the movie for your benefit alone in a darkened room, could you tell if I am running the movie forward? Or backward? Without a clock face buried in the motion picture you would be at a loss to say which way time was moving. So, I sit here in this darkened room and contemplate the existence of time in my mind and at the same time I contemplate my own life. Not knowing even if time exists. Is my life timeless? I don't think so, because at some point I will die and my life will have ended; but I do not know what direction to take with my life; forwards or backwards? If I am able to win this struggle for my own mind, I must know in which direction time moves, so that I can form the plans for the greatest battle of my life.

Time is great to use when you are late for work (and I don't even care if I go to work). Time is great to use when you are boiling a two–minute egg. Time does exist in the busy world we have created. Time is great to let you know how many minutes it is before the sun rises, and you can feel the warmth of the sun once again against your back, but actually, time is not of any use to my neurons. They just need some way to get the information that I'm wiggling my big toe with my little finger. How does such a poor dumb neuron build the complexities of a Tarantella? It's got enough trouble telling time, let alone creating the misery of my life. So, back to my life. We all have one; at least for some period of time. Some of us are happy with our life and we wear it like an old comfortable shoe; while others of us are constantly looking for newer shoes of life that may never fit.

I slowly get up and walk over to the bed; rub the back of my hand against these over–scrubbed walls and dream of days only vaguely remembered; days filled with music and the great passion that can only come from breathing life into those magic musical manuscripts written by inspired minds. Other musicians, like me want to feel the beloved passionate, sad, joyous and thrilling experience of music. In some ways, our human condition is music; it's filled with emotion and feeling and tragedy and triumph and touching each other and looking for the comfort of shared experience and sameness.

Part of my brain, at least the part that shares one of my realities, is thinking of those times before the Tarantella. Those times that existed when I had but one human reality. I didn't worry about time back then, except to use it in tiny pieces and to fill each piece with the excitement of life and the curiosity and wonderment of youth. If I shut my eyes tightly and don't breathe very deeply, I can just hear my mother calling to me across the grass, "Are you alright? It's time to eat." I can hear the soft whinnying of my horse in the distance. I can feel the soft furry touch of my cat pushing against my leg and begging for attention, and I can still feel the sweet, gentle, interrupted breezes of midday. I stand there in my mind, pulling these sensations around me like a comforting blanket, knowing that my world is safe and at the same time, making plans for those pieces of time not yet used, before the sun leaves and my shadow–day drifts into remembrance.

I was the second of three children. My early years were an adventure in learning. Many nights, because my father's work often required long hours, my mother, who worked with my father, would bring my brother, my sister and I to the office, where my sister and I would set up camp beneath the conference table when it was not being used. My father's office lent itself to family gatherings in the evening. Because of his executive position in the company he worked in a large L-shaped office, which consisted of his private work area and a conference area where he could receive visitors and hold meetings. My father's office was separated from the rest of the institute staff, by a secretary, who made sure that my father could have privacy when it was needed. My learning here was not like one gets in school. My learning consisted of occupying a special space under my father's conference room table, late into the night, wanting desperately to go home to my bed, but listening with one ear to discussions that dealt with economics and biology, the overcrowding of cities and the problems of constructing a new metropolis where none existed before. My father was the head of what we euphemistically call a Think Tank. He worked on projects ranging from satellite research to the growth of large cities. The majority of the scientists that worked in this institute were Ph.D.'s and represented more than twenty-seven different disciplines. I shared my conference table space with my younger sister Wendy, who would often crawl in next to me in our special place under the conference table and placing her head in my lap, would soon fall asleep.

My brother, who was three years older than myself, was of course too grown-up to share our special world, and so he would sit directly at the conference table and share fully, the conversations that passed between my parents and other visitors to this special spot in my father's office. While there, we were exposed to Fuzzy Sets and the world of Gödel and the struggle to compare inordinable entities, mixed in with tales of travel to exotic places and I strained to understand the throaty lisping words of a Nobel Prize winning mathematician and the bizarre sounds of poetry yet to be published. Sometimes our conference table world became a party center and we would have a cake, with little more than ten minutes between visitors, to celebrate a birthday. I did not always follow the conversations I overheard but I did absorb some life lessons, which would help me in the difficult days that would be brought about by the machinations of my disordered mind. I learned that you should not speak knowingly about a subject you do not understand and that you should respect friendship and treasure the gift of loyalty. I learned that failure is merely an invitation to try again in a new way. In essence, I developed the character that I would need an abundance of, later in my life's struggles. I learned to accept that there was more than one way to solve a problem and that it was not a tragedy to seek the advice of others. That part of my conference table world was mostly intellectual but there were other experiences that helped me to gain a balance in my life between emotion and objectivity.

When my parents were not struggling with ideas, they were making music. My mother played the harp and my father played the piano. Sometimes my parents would play four hand Ravel and Debussy at home, while smiling and laughing about some lack of coordination, or who hit which wrong note first. My brother was once a serious cellist, who had dreams someday of becoming a concert performer. He was also a composer and when we were at home, he would often treat us in his youth, to his newest composition or some ad hoc piece which he would present for the family's approval. My family would often play quintets consisting of cello, harp, flute, recorder and piano. We were, in every way, a close family of explorers of ideas and the makers of music. When I was not encamped under my father's conference table, I was in school or at home in our house in the country. My country world was very different from my office world, and between the joys of those two different places, my life was full.

I was happy in these two worlds, easily moving from one to the other. I had not yet grown to the age where friends and school activities would draw me away from my parents' work. I was reticent to leave my special place in my office world, but I was eventually drawn into an exciting place that awaits every young woman. This growing into womanhood, for me, would take place when I was about fourteen years of age, when I discovered the thrill of school plays, making music and of course, boys. But before these grand events could happen, I was to experience the first great tragedy of my young life.

My remembrances of happier days stop here, as I am reminded of that great tragedy and of the other tragedies that have led me to this dark place. I try to think once again of only those happy moments that can still give me comfort and bring me to a safe place. I begin to move my head back and forth, trying to remove that horrible day from my mind, which brought my brother's dream of being a cellist to an end. I try not to remember how near death is to all of us, hovering just out of sight, waiting to touch us and take us from this world, with our dreams yet to be fulfilled and our loves yet to be satisfied. Despite my efforts, the images slowly begin to fill my mind. I remember my parents were moving from Northridge California to the Santa Barbara area. I remember that my parents had left my brother and sister and myself with my mother's parents for safekeeping, while they attended to some final details of moving. I remember the day was very bright and I was happy to be with my grandparents whom I loved very much. My brother had decided to ride his new bike across the street to a friend's house. He was nine at the time and I was six. My grandparents lived in the country and had but a single road that passed by their house. Who would ever imagine that a quiet country road could represent such a danger to my brother? I remember that day, my mind being filled with the normal plans of a six year old: to swim in my grandparent's pool and later in the afternoon, play with a set of fascinating wooden blocks that my grandmother kept, so we could build our own towns, houses and bridges, on her living room floor. I remember I had used about half of the blocks to build my special town when I was startled by my grandmother. I had never seen her move so quickly through the house. Even though I was only six, I could feel a real fear gripping my stomach.

I yelled at my grandmother, "What's the matter?" as I watched her rush back out of the house. Her arms were filled with towels and without answering me she ran towards the back door. I jumped from the couch and ran to follow her and she screamed back at me "Stay in the house, don't come outside, I don't want you outside!"

I tentatively pushed the screen door open to see where she had gone and could see that she was kneeling down in the middle of the street. Alarmed, I ran to see what she was doing and when I got close I froze in fear. I saw my brother lying on the pavement, his head moving from side to side, softly moaning. I looked down the road and could see his mangled bike and a car, in the distance, turned over on its side. Next to the car, a woman was crying. I looked back at my brother and called his name, looking for any response from his battered body. Blood was rising from a large cut on his forehead and his skull seemed grossly misshapen. My grandfather pushed through the crowd of people that now encircled my brother's body and with one forceful motion of his hand, he pushed me aside and yelled at me to return to the house. The severity of my brother's injuries began to sink into my young brain and I ran back to the house crying uncontrollably. Once back in the house, I ran to the living room window and watched the ambulance take my brother away. I waited anxiously for my parents to arrive. I wanted to run to them and tell them what had happened, but after a short conversation with my grandfather out in the driveway, my parents immediately left for the hospital.

My parents would tell me later of their shock and their struggle, as their son lay unconscious in a hospital bed with his eyes partly open, scanning unconsciously back and forth without seeing anything. My parents sat there waiting for him to recover consciousness and hoping that he would be a whole person once again. They immediately began twelve-hour shifts, so that one of them would always be available if he regained consciousness. They told me later of those long shifts, when they would sit quietly in a chair by the bed, looking for any sign from his constantly scanning eyes. My brother remained in a coma for over two weeks, and we found out later that he had hemorrhaged significantly within his brain and could easily have died. My mother spent many months teaching my brother slowly and painfully those things he had lost due to his accident. She would patiently repeat to him, over and over again, "No, one plus one is not three, Todd, please try again". She would then reintroduce him to the reading he once knew so well; trying to re–teach a gifted child those things that were obvious to him when he was three. Nevertheless, my mother continued to teach his injured brain to learn those things once again; things that he had already taken for granted before the accident. I watched my mother day after day, calmly and patiently, teach my injured brother to get along once more in life. Sitting by her side during these days taught me the true meaning of caring. In the doing of this extended lesson, my mother also taught me perseverance and bravery in the face of adversity and she unknowingly transferred to me strength of character that would help me later in my life. My mother, an artist and writer, who endured the many deaths that accompanied her grand mal seizures, was a testament to the endurance and strength of the human will. Most importantly, she taught me that there is an innate resilience and strength in the human condition, which can enable one to recover from the worst types of adversity. My brother illuminated this message for me by continuing his music composition with a fiery determination and enthusiasm that belied the fact that he could no longer pursue his dream of becoming a concert cellist; his brain injury had affected his motor functions and took from him the delicate facility and control required to draw great music from his instrument.

I feel tears for my brother's lost hopes, but he has also shown me the strength to respond to my own adversity. My thoughts once again are interrupted as a light flashes across the room. For a moment my hospital room takes on its own life and appears to reflect the intense pain that fills my mind. It is as though the moon is shining through the windowless wall to let my mind reach for the stars once again. For a tiny instant I am reminded of the beauty of life and feel a slight spark of hope. The moving light reminds me that nurses are walking by, checking each patient's room, one by one, breaking the narrow stream of light shining through my room's window. The walking back and forth of the nurse reminds me of the movements of adults in my father's office as we viewed the legs of visitors walking past us, and my thoughts drift back to my father's office.

I would wait till my sister was asleep and would briefly crawl out from under the conference table shelter to join my brother around the table and enter into the conversations my parents would have about the day's events. I wasn't at all bothered by the fact that an hour earlier this same conference table had been filled with military men, two and three star generals and experts in every field that one could imagine.

Dinner companions at my father's office sometimes included our Xerox man who had spent most of his years arguing art along the sidewalk cafés of Paris. This man was also a sometime poet, with a gift for the sounds and feelings of words coupled together sensitively. However, they did not mix well with the consumption of alcohol, which he found to be his personal weakness in life and rendered him dependent on the kindness of others far too often for his independent nature. Another frequent guest at dinner was an ex-professor of English, who taught me to listen to the sounds of words and not just their meanings. He would speak in even tones about everything from his experiences with his brother-in-law, the Beatle Paul McCartney, to his excitement in discovering the Pulitzer prize winning book, Gödel, Escher, Bach. This was not an everyday occurrence and this was not my everyday life, but this was a part of my youthful existence, which opened my mind to many versions of the truth and to the many ways of looking at a particular problem. I learned here to grapple with an idea and to play with it and struggle with it until I could shape it into something that I could speak about with some facility.

My family sought the peace and quiet of the countryside when they were away from the office, so that I could have the best of two worlds; one filled with the excitement of technology and industry and the other filled with the openness and warmth of an unfettered sun, not striated by the shadows of tall buildings. When I was home in the country, I dreamed the dreams that every small child has about her special pet or the unexpected visits of friends and loved ones; or the times spent watching the little silken lid of a trap door spider open and watch it feel haltingly with its front legs to capture its own special version of Thanksgiving dinner. I would play with my favorite cat in front of our house or anxiously wait to bridle my horse so that I could fly across the pastures to places I had not visited before.

Overlaid on my two worlds, like a frosted blanket covering the two layers of a magnificent cake, was the constant music that my parents created and listened to. This music filled the air with images of dark forests and heroism. Whether mom and dad were creating something intellectual or arguing the finer points of a technical construction, in the background there was the clarity of Bach, the roughened turmoil of Beethoven and the sweet lyricism of Chopin. To me these worlds were woven together through the strong threads of a tapestry of music, which clarified my thoughts and framed my life. It was the soothing comment. It was the subtle conclusion. It was the beautiful lullaby that tied together the unending complexities of words and pictures and plans and actions that were my parent's life in those formative years.

The measure of my mind's breadth, were the thinking spaces inserted into my mind to yield a sensitivity to unsolved problems. The edge of that same ruler, gave me the ability to make plans and draw conclusions that were both objective in their logic and subjective in the texture of their emotional context.

I was fourteen and my body was feeling the changes of a maturity that was not quite there. My mind was growing mentally, giving me a balance between my thoughts about the world and the response of my body to those thoughts. It was in the middle of this growth and the excitement of these two worlds that I experienced the first hint of my brain's disorder. Even before I was exposed to the unnerving saw-toothed reality of delusions and the blinding numbness of depression, I came face to face with a new reality. It happened one evening in my bedroom, deep within the dark weavings of sleep. I had been awakened to the quiet darkness of my room. I remember looking briefly at my clock, keeping its usual vigil over my blanket-covered sleep. I sat up slowly, thinking that someone had entered my room, perhaps to check on some nocturnal sound that I had not been aware of. I noticed a figure standing in the corner of my room, silently folding clothes and placing them ever so carefully in that neat kind of structure known only to the practiced hands of a woman used to caring for other's needs; placing them just so, so that the user could easily find them and select the neatly ironed parts of this clothed ode to a life of caring for others. I looked closer at the figure, who worked so quietly, thinking that it might be my mother trying to move ahead of the day's chores during my sleep. As she turned to face me, she smiled a slow, gentle smile as though to comfort me and to urge me to return to the sweet arms of sleep. I realized at that moment that I was looking at my father's mother whose lap I had often sat upon when I was younger. I also remembered in that terrible moment that she was dead. She had died two years earlier. I felt disoriented and yet thankful to see her once again. I did not realize fully, at that time, what my mind had just conjured. I did not understand what else it would bring to my life in the future, or that it would blur the boundaries of my reality. I laid back down, following her soft instructions, and fell asleep once more.

My maturing mind had now within its inner rooms a growing new type of reality, which I would soon learn was filled with more than the gentle image of my grandmother. In a few days, I put this vision aside and again was filled with the excitement of new discovery that gives youth that special sensitivity to the smell and feel of the earth, the library odors which escape when one opens a book read many times, and the loving touch of a mother's hand, brushing the wayward hairs away from your face, in that silent gesture that says we are together and I love you very much.

Over time, I faded from my office world and entered into more lively conversations with my friends and excited discussions about the latest school play. Still there were conversations around the dinner table with my family, in which I continued to stretch my mentality, touching the sky with my mind while feeling the warm emotions of love with my body. This was a time when I could ask questions about life without embarrassment and where I dared to pontificate about facts I felt I knew, while receiving a depth of questions which would have been absent from any of my local school examinations. This is where I learned the difference between the hard questions and the easy questions; about life and the living of it; and existence and the meaning that existence has for us all. This is where I learned of the many ways one can look at the same apparently simple problem and consider the fact that there is not always just one solution and that the answer to a question can be multiple questions without an answer.

But for all the technical squabbling and intellectual arguments at home, above it all I remember the rising sounds of music, constantly reminding me that my truest love was the flute. It is small wonder, looking back, that I could have ever considered communicating the messages of my life through any other means than the beautiful flute and the sounds that I learned to generate, as I grew out of that exciting mixture of intellect, soul and emotion.

My thoughts return to the dark room of this hospital; to moments already lived, to pain first felt as my brain began its construction of an alternate reality. Those memories of days long past are mostly crowded out now by a reality that leaves little room for kind remembrances. I try once again to think of those happier days, but they seem hollow to me now and faded like the old sounds of the train whistle, opening the quiet night as it moves through town. Still, those days were the development of my body, the birth of my soul and the construction of my brain's special reality.

I remember how early I learned that music meant emotion, experience and love to me personally; how I discovered the importance of music is an epiphany I shall always remember and cherish. But, it would take more growth and years of work before that illuminating experience. If life is nothing else, it is a long trail of coupled experiences, and the richness of each experience that is bounded only by the depth of one's soul. When you're young, and have yet to feel the many experiences of adulthood, you cherish those discoveries that have helped you to grow a tiny bit and refine the structure of that grand emergent characteristic we call mind. It was one of these kinds of experiences that first introduced me to the deep resonance of music within my being.

How I wish I could recapture that moment when I first discovered my flute. I shut my eyes and think back to that exciting day. It started out simply enough, in a band room with an empty floor. I remember as the local music store representative came to the room and emptied a truckload of instruments for lease or purchase onto that shiny wooden floor. I stared in wonder and excitement at this enormous assortment of instruments; cases purposely positioned wide open, revealing sparkling shades of brass, silver and gold. Needless to say, the instrument salesman had generated the desired effect; all over the band room, there were children pulling excitedly at their parent's shirtsleeves, pointing at the instrument they "had to have". I scanned the entire room, searching for the instrument that was made for me. My eyes quickly settled on the shiniest instruments in the room, a row of ten brand new flutes. I was immediately attracted to the flute's delicate design and the precious silver metal with which they were forged. When someone handed me one of those shiny silver flutes, and asked me if I would like to try to make music with this instrument, I immediately fell in love. I was eleven years old. The sight of this instrument was so overwhelming to me, that I just stared quietly for a long period at this new object held in my lap. I heard someone behind me say, "Try it, it's a flute". I picked it up and felt its weight and enjoyed the shine of its polished surface and my hands slowly ran over the many keys protruding from this new, unique and exciting device. Its beauty intrigued me and I felt the excitement that a young child feels when given a new object to discover and enjoy. That first scene is still so real and vivid in my mind, that I can see it as though in a theater, watching the projection of my experiences flow in front of me, uninterrupted. Later in the day, I was told I could take the flute home with me. (Not knowing my parents had purchased it).

When I got home I ran to my room and opened the flute case, marveling at its beauty, I carefully placed rods and tenons together and my heart beat faster, as I put the embouchure plate to my lips and blew softly into the flute. A loud note sounded and I shook with pride and excitement. By bedtime I had learned the C Major scale and as I fell asleep that night, I envisioned myself on the concert stage, my flute glistening in the bright lights as I performed a solo piece in front of a large audience. This was the beginning of my journey as a concert musician. Of course this was not yet my greatest epiphany, it was still myself and the flute as two separate beings, strange to each other and too timid to be introduced more completely. It would take many hours and many years for me to make this flute my companion and the instrument of my passion.

Art of course, is not just a matter of simple emotion or deep feeling, it consists of control and skill, and an understanding of those elements that are needed to come together to produce true beauty. It takes more than inner feelings to project those emotions we all deeply strive to appreciate or to feel, through the use of an instrument that is not part of our own bodies. It was in fact, many years later that I had the true epiphany which was the deep understanding of the meaning of music in my life and my all–consuming desire to communicate the depth of my emotions to others.

I remember all of this as though it was happening now in this quiet dark room. I feel the excitement of the moments before I placed that special instrument to my lips and began to play the Bach Suite in b minor. I had prepared for this piece as I had countless other pieces in long arduous rehearsals, weighing the sound and the meaning of each note separately and feeling the expression of groups of these notes as though they were my thoughts winding through the maze of my being to be sent out to all those who would hear and share the sounds. I remember the hall that I played in left just enough time for my sounds to fill the space and form an architecture of musical beauty which held its place above the heads of the audience, crystal clear, sonorous, and with all the meaning which it had when it left my lips. I could probably tell you all of the details of that day and maybe I will when I am less tired, but for me, it made my vision of the world clearer, defined my future goals, and defined my path from youth to membership in humankind. This experience was profound and changed my feelings towards my music and my life forever.

I feel a slight chill, and it breaks the stream of thoughts, letting in the sounds once again of the quiet sobs from the room next door. How did I get here? It has been such an insidious descent into this cold, stark room. The quiet sobbing from the next room stops and the silence blankets my senses. Now I am truly alone, not even a faint sob to keep me company. Alone with my thoughts in this protective, yet intrusive place, the ambivalence over whether to live or die divides my fatigued mind. Despite the thick fog that has settled within my sedated consciousness, I grope for a pleasant thought, a thought that will provide me with even the tiniest light from within this dark space in which I currently reside. The sobbing in the room next to me resumes and my mind turns dark, like the last ember in a fire that had long ago come to the quiet end of its time. I look to my mind once more in blame and anger. It's capable of giving me all the thoughts that I need to direct the talent in my muscles when I finger my flute and it's broad enough to keep me out of trouble when I stray from carefully made plans. Which part of this mind that I contemplate, has brought me to this place? Which neurons should I blame for this destruction of my reality? I don't know any of these answers, but I feel I must continue to ask the question. Maybe this is a question whose only answer is more questions.

I have gone through many experiences by this stage in my life and my body has felt them, my emotions have been shaped by them and my mind has recorded them, just as they might be found in the far corner of their own dust filled library, and placed them just so, next to worn leather covered memories of arithmetic and reading. The joys of Seven Story Mountain and the anguish of Death In Venice; all are free to mingle in my mind with the music of Taffenel/Gaubert studies and Marcel Moyse. The great geometric construction of the neurons in my cortices play an ever increasing complexity of notes in disharmony with the amygdala and hippocampus that I so desperately need, to maintain my proper emotional context, and the evenness of my so–called life in art. Like Berlioz, I so desperately want to feel all of the emotions of life, and I know that my mind must lead me to the true alter where I will be one with my instrument.

My mind wants to remember back to other times again, times that were more clearly defined for me and in which I can still seek comfort and solace, but for now the fuzzy distortion of thoughts created by the numerous medications circulating through my brain, makes it difficult to ponder such questions anymore. Will my mind continue to reassemble itself in strange new ways in this desolate place? My mind struggles to continue with these thoughts but I no longer control its obtuse and illogical meanderings. I try once again to cover my mind with the framework of better times, so as to bind together the loosening girders and widening structures of my increasingly disordered mind. I squeeze my eyelids ever tighter together to conjure up those warm memories, as I drift back into a troubled reverie but can only think of those dark early moments in which my mind turned against me.

I wish I had my music to comfort me in this awful space; even a plaintive solo melody would be welcome. Just to hold my flute once again would be a comfort to me, the shiny silver and white–gold luminous against the blue velvet of its protective home, but here there is only empty silence and the well scrubbed walls of nurses long past. I wonder if their hopes and dreams were fulfilled? I wonder what this empty space meant to them?

A nurse knocks quietly on the door, opens it briefly and walks away. For a moment, in this isolated room, I can almost hear a faint strain of the final bars of Griffes Poem, but my mind cannot hold onto the previous sounds; and like trying to hold water in my bare hands, the impressionist sounds drain away. By now I have climbed back into the hospital bed. I turn over and bury my body under the cold institutional covers; my cheeks taut from tears that have dried on my face. I hear scratching in the walls again. Perhaps the spiders have found me. I am ashamed of what a coward I have become. How could I perform in front of thousands of people but not be able to face my own mind? How will I endure? Gradually, my thoughts drift to a much happier time in my life, when my music making grew into an all–consuming passion.

The art of making music was intoxicating and powerful. I discovered that every emotion experienced by a human being could be captured and communicated through musical phrases. Music became my first language; nothing was more fulfilling than being able to communicate my feelings and emotions through a controlled series of dynamics, articulations, keys, and time signatures. My days were filled with; scales, arpeggios, etudes, studies, tone exercises, breathing exercises, sight singing, music theory, music history, small ensemble work, large ensemble work, master classes, workshops and private lessons. It had been two years since I received my first flute. By thirteen years of age I had already found a music teacher, who performed with the Santa Barbara Symphony. I studied with her for a short time and then switched to someone who was famous in his day as a concert flutist and began studies with him. He was gruff in his attitude but was a skilled technician and he began to teach me the very specialized technique I would need to become a concert flutist. I was still thirteen when I auditioned for first chair in the Santa Barbara Junior Symphony. I prepared for this audition for weeks, learning the top twenty five orchestral excerpts and one solo piece which was required by the audition committee. To my surprise, I won the audition and was given first chair in the orchestra. A year after winning my position as first chair in the junior symphony, I auditioned for the Santa Barbara Junior Symphony Concerto

Competition and won first place. I was awarded a solo performance with the orchestra, and I was thrilled. I was fourteen at the time and I was about to play my first concerto in front of a live audience.

Now my career began to blossom. I was awarded a series of various scholarships for performance, first by the Scandinavian Foundation and then by the Pillsbury Foundation. These are nationwide grants awarded through competition to gifted musicians. I went on to win a Santa Barbara Foundation award which consisted of a granting of money and a Santa Barbara Music Club Scholarship.

As these various successes continued, I entered and won The Santa Barbara Symphony Young Soloist Competition at the age of fifteen. All of these days of hard work and mechanics since I had first picked up that shiny flute when I was eleven, had paid off and I now could prepare for my debut before a large audience with a major orchestra. I spent months preparing the compositions I would play and memorized every note until I could repeat them to myself each night before I went to bed. I rehearsed with my accompanist for weeks, until I was ready to solo. I was going to be the featured soloist in concert with the Santa Barbara Symphony and as I stood on stage in front of this great orchestra, delivering my performance of the Gluck Concerto in G Major, I felt completely at home. As the resonant sounds of my flute coupled with the orchestra behind me, a delicate marriage of sounds was created. As my solo line weaved in and out of the harmonies created by the strings, I could hear the unique voice of my flute, hovering over the orchestral accompaniment and reverberating back to me from the last rows of the theatre.

As I hit the last note, the applause of the thousands of people who were there washed over me and I could feel nothing else. I bowed. More applause. I continued to bow. I fell in love with the art of music performance. This was my music. This was my life.

2

The Refrain of Love's Lost

Overtures to Anguish

Application to the New England Conservatory of Music was for me the beginning of my adult life. It meant leaving the home where I was born, separation from my family and the maturation of my musical abilities. But before I could make this right of passage, I had to take part in a stringent audition which was to be held at The Dorothy Chandler Pavilion in Los Angeles. My sister, who also wished to attend NEC accompanied me to the audition. We both completed our auditions for acceptance without fanfare. The auditions were done in a large empty room with only our parents and accompanists present and recorded by a representative from New England Conservatory and couriered back to New England Conservatory for review by their acceptance committee. After waiting anxiously for weeks with great anticipation, we were informed of not only our acceptance but also of scholarships we had been awarded.

I was poised for this next phase of my musical development. My sister and I were going to the country's oldest independent school of music, and we could not wait to begin this new adventure. I was now entering an institution which could complete the marriage of understanding between myself and my instrument.

I said tearful goodbyes to my parents who had come to see the conservatory with me, and I felt a twinge of panic that I had not experienced in years as I watched them drive away. The conservatory's buildings were old and well used by a long stream of great musicians, giving it an elegance that only maturity can achieve. The conservatory was the home of Jordan Hall, which had heard the glorious sounds of such great musicians as Pablo Casals, Arthur Rubenstein, Isaac Stern, Julius Baker, Benny Goodman, Yo–Yo Ma and many others.

I took a brief look at the rehearsal rooms with their thick white acoustic board and noted the universality of those rooms where a musician must face his own instrument, alone and unaided, in order to achieve that harmony which comes only from solitary insights, isolated from the real world.

In many ways, those practice rooms bear a frightening resemblance to the quiet rooms I have seen in this hospital, except that in this hospital, I have no instrument, except my mind upon which to play the music of my madness. At least the room that I am in, shelters me from the noises and busy movement of the nurses at their station and allows me to contemplate my life with the solitude that I need. My thoughts drift back, once again, to the conservatory. It took longer than anticipated to get completely settled and we anxiously looked forward to our first dinner away from home. Dining in the cafeteria was always a journey of discovery. We learned quickly that we had to not only select food carefully, but also examine it thoroughly as though on a safari, to make sure that no parts of the food were moving inappropriately on the plate. Gravy on meat often had a lumpiness that we could not always attribute to un–dissolved flour. We found out later that food in this cafeteria required not only a studied approach, but also much action of the fork, fingers and knife to separate the dead parts from the live parts.

Breakfast was even more of an epiphany, in which one discovered that products made from a mix such as muffins or pancakes might contain even more protein than the recommended daily allowance printed on the box. This is not to say that the food was insect ridden, but we were often witness to Olympic events in which the participants were mainly cockroaches taking part in synchronous swimming in the punch, while others aimed for gold medals in the pancake broad jumping event. Not only were there cockroaches, but the cafeteria itself became an Archipelago in which crawling, floating and flying creatures evolved in an environment aptly suited for their accelerated evolution. We became very selective in our choice of the gourmet foods available to us, making sure that our choices contained at least as many refined ingredients as the manufacturer had intended.

It was interesting when we took our portions of cereal in the morning. The cereal was administered from a large flexible bag, with a handle on the side, which you could turn, and in return it would pour into your bowl a pre-measured amount of breakfast cereal. The only problem was that on some occasions, when you took your portion of cereal you received an added dollop of insectoid parts or a completely intact cockroach, ready and willing to share your breakfast with you. Fortunately, they did not always bring their cousins with them, leaving enough food for me to complete my breakfast, although with such guests, community dining took on a whole new meaning.

My thoughts are wrenched back to my room in the hospital as I hear scratching on the wall from spiders heard but unseen. The terror grips me and ends my stream of consciousness. I look upward but see no apparent source. The nurse opens the door briefly and looks in to see that I am in bed and shuts it again, leaving me alone once more with the thoughts of my misshapen life. My mind momentarily blanks out the noises of the spiders and returns to more pleasant times in New England and that great conservatory.

It was Christmas time now, three months since I had entered this new stage of my learning and I flew home for the holidays. Upon my return to Boston I had to fly out of Los Angeles Airport. Little did I know it would give me a chance to perform with my instrument and pass on its love to none other than a security guard and a small audience who had not paid admission. I remember entering the airport and when a security guard saw my flute on the x-ray machine, he mistakenly thought it was a weapon. I told the guard that I was a music student and he was simply looking at a flute in its case, but the anxious guard did not believe me, so I asked if I could open the case and show it to him. As people around us started to stare at the commotion, I slowly opened the case and assembled my flute. I was incredulous when the guard asked me to play something to prove that it was indeed a musical instrument. So I lifted the flute to my mouth, while he snidely asked if I took requests. I ignored his question and proceeded to play the flute solo from Prokofiev's Peter and the Wolf, over the racket caused by the loud noises of the airport. As soon as I finished playing, I could hear applause coming from the many on–lookers who had gathered to watch "the show" and the guard sheepishly thanked me for the "concert" and passed me through security. By this point in my life, I had played many concerts and received applause from many strangers, but this experience was very up close and personal. Although I did not know the guard, nor any of the people who stood by and applauded, I realized at that moment, the full power that my music had to transmit its beautiful message to other human beings, even in as unlikely a place as a busy airport.

After I returned to my dormitory I met with a few of my friends to discuss our holidays at home, when I experienced the paralyzing fear of a panic attack. I tried to douse the fire of anxiety by simply ignoring it, but this was one panic attack that would not be refused its place in the limelight. I learned later that these attacks of anxiety, although painful enough in their own right, were merely harbingers of the depression and delusions that later would become part of my alternate reality. I quickly made an excuse to my friends that I had to go study and fled to my room. I was shaking as I unlocked my door and went inside. I hoped to see my sister but she had not returned from practicing yet. I sat on my bed rocking back and forth as the waves of panic mercilessly racked my body again and again. The powerful exposition of my mind's discordant fugue had begun and many atonal sounds were to follow, disrupting my mind with a new alternate reality.

I had panic attacks everywhere after that. Everything and nothing seemed to trigger them and each successive panic attack was worse than the one before. There was no obvious reason underlying these attacks and no special actions that I could tell that would bring them on or make them better. Every day became a struggle just to survive. I would live hour-to-hour sometimes making silent deals with myself, as I tried any mind game I could, to survive another class or rehearsal without having to leave, due to unbearable panic. I had no control over the powerful statements of anxiety that would play themselves out in my mind. I endured the attacks in secret; a quiet overture of anguish.

After weeks of panic attacks, something even more sinister moved from out of the depths of my mind, to cover my body and my soul with the darkness of deep depression. My mind was playing out the overture to the music of my madness. It had but one movement left to play and that was the delusions that soon would fill the inner rooms of my mind. This depression was settling over me like a cold, gray fog. It surrounded my visions of brighter times with a murkiness which I could not dissipate.

I sometimes busied my weary mind with thoughts of others in more pain than myself. I became friends with a fellow student who suffered such pain. Her name was Elizabeth. She was a fellow instrumental student in her junior year. She lived on the same floor as I and I soon noticed that she would take what looked like horse hobbles into the shower with her. I found out later that she had multiple sclerosis. We had a number of long talks about her MS and she told me that she had a fairly advanced case and was completely numb from the waist down. In these conversations she showed not only strength of character but also a great interest in life itself. She would remind me of how beautiful life can be when one is able to see it clearly without the shroud of great depression. She had serious respiratory problems which exhibited themselves as a breathless sound as she tried to speak and find sufficient air to complete her thought. The symptoms of Elizabeth's disease would sometimes hide themselves, waiting for an opportunity, when she least expected it, to jump upon her hapless body and force the very air out of her lungs until she would find herself on the brink of respiratory arrest. In spite of all this, she played the French Horn with a brilliance and mastery belying the difficulties her disease brought with it. And still, she showed the optimism to hope for completion of one more year in the conservatory. In talking with her, I could sense the nearness of death which remains invisible to most of us, but which to her was a clarified silhouette remaining in full sight.

I too felt this reality of the nearness of death through my experiences with Elizabeth. Although my mind would later bring me to consider terminating my own life; here was a victim who had no choice as to whether she lived or died and yet smiled with the passing of each day. I stayed close to her, as a student sitting next to her master, trying to learn the true lessons of existence and the braveness of facing life's uncertainties.

I remember vividly in shades of black and gray, this shadow of a person desperately banging on my door in early evening. I could sense the desperateness of the knock. I opened the door and could sense the figure of death hiding behind her slim silhouette. Elizabeth's smile was gone from her face. Her skin had a grayish cast. She was obviously struggling for air. Her eyes had the frantic movement of a young deer caught away from its home, panicked and not knowing which way to run. She breathlessly told me she had tried all of her inhalers, but nothing was working. She said to me in an almost growling voice that summed up her desperateness, "I need medical attention immediately, but I can't find a cab". I reached for the phone, without even thinking of the full seriousness of the situation and called for an ambulance. Almost as an automaton she mindlessly grabbed my arm, as though hoping to keep from slipping over that ominous cliff where death waited. She whispered to me with what little breath she had, "There is no more time". I rushed her with me to the ground floor where I found a cab and quickly took her to Deaconess Hospital. The triage nurse at the hospital met us with cool indifference and ignored my pleas for immediate help. Elizabeth was far too weak to fight for the right treatment and so she sat there next to me, motionless, waiting for either her deliverance or her death. I soon found myself shouting for help from anyone. My screams for help brought nurses to quiet me down and as they were attending to my angry and hysterical commands, Elizabeth quietly collapsed to the floor. She lay there in silence as the first nurse to reach her whispered, "She is not breathing". My heart and my mind were numb to the full depth of what was happening. I hoped that my thoughts could support her as her apparently lifeless body waited for assistance. After what seemed to be many long minutes, I saw the doctors trying to resuscitate Elizabeth. They lifted her body onto a gurney and whisked her down the corridor away from me as I dazedly watched her disappear into the inner rooms of the hospital. I sat in the waiting room quietly, with the thoughts of my own panic and destructive fears and contemplated the richness of life, which I could still have, if I had the courage to fight for it. This opportunity for a long life had been denied to Elizabeth. Death was not only in view, but he held her special gift just out of reach. Finally one of the doctors walked slowly toward me and told me that Elizabeth had been resuscitated and was resting comfortably in her room. I said a silent prayer to my God and hoped that Elizabeth could at least live out her dream of one more year in the conservatory. I asked a nurse how to find Elizabeth's room and quickly walked there. She was sitting partly upright in her bed with her head leaning deeply into the pillow giving her support. Her face looked whiter than I had ever seen it before. She was using a lung inhaler and one could see a light mist rising from the device as it sat in her mouth. Upon my entering the room she slowly looked in my direction and momentarily removed the inhaler from her mouth. Looking concerned, she asked me in that breathless voice that I knew so well, if I was O.K. I was awestruck that this person, lying in front of me, could endure such adversity and still ask if I was all right. If it was possible for her to live with such adversity, surely I should be able to live with the pain of my tortured mind. I fell into bed that night vowing to defeat the strange configurations of my alternate reality. Elizabeth did not expect to live more than a few years, but I knew in my heart that the richness of her life would make it seem like decades of other's less meaningful existences. After that incident, I threw myself even harder into my music and each day I became closer to my instrument.

My flute and I were beginning to merge into one complex personality with which I could pass on my hopes and dreams to others in a wordless harmony of sounds. All this new fervent effort led me to a very special event which came about shortly after my experience with Elizabeth.

This special event was a major competition for all of the flutists in the surrounding area. It would be filled with those gifted students that filled the Boston area with music. I was anxious to see how my talents would fare in such an important competition. The name of this imposing event was The Messian Competition, named after the composer who wrote eloquent contemporary music for the flute and other instruments. The piece chosen for this competition was entitled Le Merle Noir (The Black Bird) and was filled with the challenges that only a flutist, who understands the most difficult mechanics of her instrument, can appreciate. Every flutist in the conservatory and in Boston had entered this important competition. I immediately sought the advice of my personal flute instructor, master conductor and flute player, Claude Monteux, so that we could go over the intricacies of this difficult contemporary piece. I trained for this flute and piano work for two straight months, fighting my degrading mind, while perfecting the challenging rhythms, and intervallic leaps that led to Messian's personal vision of his music for The Black Bird. The weeks flew by as I improved my interpretations of this difficult piece and became as one with my accompanist, perfecting the ensemble that Messian envisioned. It was finally time for the competition.

Audition times were posted at the conservatory and we were only given ten minutes each in which to perform the piece and impress the judges. I had placed a note on my door with my audition time highlighted in red and the night before the competition I set my alarm clock to go off a full four hours before my assigned audition time. I wanted plenty of time in the morning to warm up my fingers and lots of extra time to negotiate the three subway connections I had to make, in order to get to the competition site on time. The only thing I had not counted on was THE BEAST.

My first acquaintance with THE BEAST was my first day at the dormitory. THE BEAST was actually an elevator which had long ago required retirement but was still serving out its days dutifully, making its trip as best it could with the aid of crutches and an occasional lift from a hapless student. I met THE BEAST on my first day at school when I needed to carry my things up to my assigned room on the sixth floor. With bags heavier than I was and six flights of stairs in front of me, I decided to take the modern approach and use the elevator, knowing full well it would whisk me quickly, silently and safely to my floor, effortlessly carrying along with it all of my baggage without a moan or a comment. As I started towards the elevator, a student, clearly in at least his second year, cautioned me, "Are you planning on taking "THE BEAST" upstairs"? I looked quizzically at him and asked, "What beast"? He looked seriously back at me and said, "THE BEAST", surely you know about "THE BEAST". Actually I didn't know about THE BEAST, but I was soon to learn that taking this particular elevator was more than a mere modern convenience, it was one of the great adventures next to rowing singly in a rowboat, from the west coast of California to Hawaii. I came to understand after many unwanted stops, jerks, rumbles and other unearthly sounds, that this truly was "THE BEAST". Standing before it, one gently pushed the button and stood back to look at its gaping jaws, slowly opening. What was its intent today; to allow us safe entry to its insides only to keep us prisoners beyond time? Or would it prove once again, that it could easily stop and open its doors between floors without hesitating or apologizing? I never researched totally the archeology of "THE BEAST", but I determined that its origins began in ancient Egypt where the original designers used special sand weights and pulleys activated by secret counter balances, and a map, which led one to that special chamber for the God–king, where he could then commune with the netherworld.

The day of the Messian competition (THE COMPETITION), I pressed the button to THE BEAST and the doors slowly opened on the sixth floor, allowing me access to the ancient innards of this great deliverer. On this particular day, my hopes were high that I would reach a level of performance within this elevator far above normal, namely, arrival at the ground floor in less than three minutes of vertical travel. I expected to leave the dormitory at 8:15 am, travel effortlessly down to the first floor, grab the subway and reach the competition early and with plenty of time to warm up. I stepped gingerly onto the uneven floor and watched those great gaping jaws close out the world beyond, not knowing whether the ancient design would work its magic and take me downward to the first floor or take me for another grand visit to the depths of our special basement, so I could inhale the exotic vapors of moldy boxes and crates whose destinations had gone awry. As I glimpsed the last tiny, narrow, vertical view of the outside world, I prayed on this special day that THE BEAST would have mercy on my soul because on this special day I was to compete in the Messian competition. THE COMPETITION. Time was of the essence. I started this journey on the sixth floor with little time for stairs or any of those less modern conveniences. After all, I had accurately timed my descent as well as the rest of my trip so that I would arrive at the competition ON TIME. I had my flute bag packed, my gloves on and my accompanist waiting for me in the lobby. Little did my accompanist know that I had to enter THE BEAST to make this vast journey to the ground floor. It reminded me of the ancient trip across the river Styx, could I make it to the other side? There was no coinage to place in THE BEAST. It had no requirement to deliver me, except that the great ancients, who designed it, knew that it must make its journey to the other side when needed. With a great heaving sigh, and a low ugly growl, THE BEAST began to make its journey downward. I looked at my watch anxiously. I prayed to the God of elevators for forgiveness for all of those thoughts that I have had about THE BEAST and its makers. I felt the floor continuing to move below my feet, we had reached the fifth floor. Fortunately, THE BEAST did not stop and we continued our downward movement. "I am Free," I thought. "I am going to make it." The elevator Gods really have heard my prayers. Floor three moves by at a slow but steady pace, just two floors to go. Then I see it– floor two. That shining example of numerology, which when added to one, gives us the magic of the ancients. And now at last, floor one, the most prime of all prime numbers that I seek most in my frenzied state. THE BEAST lets out one more great creaking moan, showing that it has crossed the river and its beautiful, dull, battered doors slowly begin to open and then I feel it, the shaking of the great jaws, the weird rumblings of THE BEAST as it struggles to open its gates to set me free. My God, I can see reality, I can see my accompanist, I can see the sunshine through THE BEAST'S partly opened jaws, but the opening, alas, is too narrow. THE BEAST has finally done me in. Alas, poor BEAST, I knew him well. He had moments of glory and feats untold, but he could not cross the river Styx this one last time. Needless to say, I was PISSED. I looked at my watch again and I have twelve minutes to make it to the subway. I was going to miss THE COMPETITION. (Normally, this would not have been a tremendous problem. Not for a normal elevator.) Not for a normal day without THE COMPETITION. I was so close to success. I could see my accompanist was just inches away on the other side of the frozen doors. Normally, one would pick up a phone and call for help, and efficient engineers would be there, helping you out the door and dusting off your clothes; but not in THE BEAST. The phone lay helplessly in its nest, the phone cord dangling from the receiver, torn from its roots. My accompanist waved at me and tried to press one hand through the narrow opening of the great doors, but she could not make it. She then tried with all her might to force open the jaws of the door, but THE BEAST was dead; rigor mortis had entered the scene and stiffened every part. I lean against the door and yell for someone to "GET ME OUT OF HERE"! I have to get to "THE COMPETITION". The accompanist knew that the normal procedures did not apply to THE BEAST. The accompanist knew that special procedures were required for THE BEAST. In fact there was a special Elevator Guard House, in which a man was stationed with an over sized crowbar, which he would calmly use with great finality and gusto, to move the doors apart, allowing THE BEAST to regurgitate its occupants. But today was special. Today was THE COMPETITION. The special elevator guardsman walked resolutely towards the doors. I knew freedom must be near. He breathed a huge sigh and then took in a great intake of air, expanding his entire chest until he stood magnificently and firmly in front of those narrowly opened doors. He confidently grabbed the huge crowbar in both of his hands and then resolutely set it aside. What was he thinking? Why wasn't he trying to open the door? I could barely see him through the small vertical opening, looking down at that huge crowbar and shaking his head and then looking at the elevator and mumbling something silently to himself and then I realized the awful truth; he was going to attempt this feat of power with his bare hands, unaided by the tools of his noble trade. What an act of bravery I thought, for him to possibly sacrifice his life to save me from THE BEAST. The Guardsman slowly placed one hand on each side of the partly opened door, and his muscles rippled and bulged and strained, as he attempted to move those doors out and apart, revealing all of the reality of the ground floor to my captive eyes. I knew I'd be out in another instant. His face began to get redder and he let out a giant blast of air, which actually partly blew me back towards the rear of the frozen BEAST. With another great sigh, he began to reach resolutely for the great crowbar leaning just outside the elevator, but I heard it slowly drop sideways to the floor with a great metallic thud, possibly to never be used again. Casey had struck out. Just then three students wanting to use THE BEAST asked the breathless guard inquisitively, "Is it stuck?" The guardsman answered firmly, "Well, I'm not sure, I suppose—maybe." The three students talked quietly together as four more students, needing to use THE BEAST, gathered around asking, "What's the problem?" The guardsman said, "I think it may be stuck, I think the doors are trying to close." Another student said, "Press the button, I think the doors are trying to open." Another student said quickly, "Get a chair from the cafeteria, that always works." In the meantime, after what seemed like an eternity, two large freshmen came back with a single chair from the cafeteria and quickly inserted two of the chair's legs into the narrow opening of the elevator. The guardsman watched quizzically, as they grimly determined to part the doors. Two more students, who had just joined the growing crowd outside THE BEAST, grabbed the back of the chair and helped to push it towards the front of the elevator. With a great snapping sound, the chair legs bent and then broke, leaving one crippled chair, sixteen bewildered students, a large red faced guardsman and myself desperately desiring to escape from this prison and reach THE COMPETITION. By now, I was really worried about getting to this important contest, and I was starting to worry about my life because my blood sugar was lowering with each passing minute. I could no longer see my accompanist amongst the crowd. I tried yelling out her name, but people mistook that for a cry for help and began pushing their faces against the narrow opening of the door, asking what I needed. Someone called out for food from the cafeteria. I desperately hoped I would not be joined by the jungle of creatures infesting the food they would bring to me. The students yelled to me, "Help is on the way." I thought for sure they had found the secret to opening the doors. Instead they were handing, as though a special trophy, from one person to the next, a single large muffin from the cafeteria, to give me sustenance in my hour of need. The last person handed the muffin, quickly attempted to put the tasty morsel through the narrow opening of the doors, but in doing so crushed the huge muffin to death. Its corpse fell in small pieces to the floor, another victim of the poor, dead BEAST. The remainder of the muffin did add sustenance for my only other companion in the elevator, a rather large and wise cockroach, a former member of the basement staff, who had been trying vainly to scrape its way out of this tomb and join its family in the cafeteria. Through my now hazy thoughts about THE COMPETITION, I could feel my blood sugar dropping and I began to feel faint. I searched desperately for untouched crumbs of the muffin, but the cockroach and his cousins had claimed it all. I cried weakly for help, and some of the students rushed back to the cafeteria to bring me liquid nourishment. They knew now that the doors were frozen too close together for anything but a straw to penetrate, so they brought me some orange juice, which I gratefully accepted by sucking on the straw. Finishing the orange juice, I breathed a sigh of relief and asked feebly for "SOMEONE TO CALL THE FIRE DEPARTMENT, BEFORE I MISS THE DAMN COMPETITION"! This last, desperate cry for help must have gotten through, because within the next few minutes, every single male from the first three floors of the dorm, positioned himself to face squarely, the stiffened, unyielding jaws of THE BEAST. Soon, instead of the red helmets of firemen, I saw countless hands of trombonists, violinists, bass players, and every other imaginable musician, grasping the doors. With the strength of the lesser Gods, known only to the Great Elevator Keeper In The Sky, they began to slowly widen the narrow opening of those ancient doors. With a groan that must have come from below the dustiest box in that old basement, the doors began to slowly move apart. At last I was free. The students cheered. I grumbled something about being late and with one sideways glance at the guardsman, who now stood exhausted and motionless, I signaled to my accompanist and left the building.

Epilogue: The adventure over, I was thirty minutes late, but the judges made special arrangements for my entry, knowing that I had done battle with THE BEAST and had won. And miracle–of–miracles I actually tied for first place.

Post Epilogue: I realize that I have made some comments about New England Conservatory which may not be appreciated by the present staff or administration, most of this outside the descriptions of my illness, have been written tongue and cheek and should be accepted as such. I left New England Conservatory with great sorrow and miss the exciting atmosphere which it extends to all young musicians. Consider these descriptions only a verbal Valentine sending kudos and thanks to a great institution that I deeply admire.

With the Messian Competition over, and the thrill of winning still fresh in my mind, I still felt the uneasiness of my depression returning. Even though I was succeeding in my musical career, life was becoming increasingly difficult. My depression and my panic attacks, although strangers at first, coupled to form an insidious combination, leaving me with both devastating panic and deep depression. This terrible duet of moods stripped from my personality and my world, the intense joy and satisfaction I received from performing my music. I began to dread rehearsals and school in general. Any specific situation in which I was required to maintain my stability, such as in a class or a rehearsal, became an impossibility. I constantly felt trapped as though in a room so small I could not stretch my arms outward or take more than one step in any direction. The joy I received from sharing my gift of music had all but vanished.

After much anguished consideration, I decided to leave New England Conservatory and attend the University of California in Santa Barbara because it was closer to home and the support of my parents. I left New England Conservatory with some misgivings and great sorrow, but because of my degrading mental condition I felt that this was the best compromise possible.

I started at UCSB at the age of twenty, with much hope for actively continuing my music career. UCSB was a very different atmosphere from New England Conservatory because it consisted of students in a wide range of disciplines other than music. I had an opportunity to make friends who were majoring in the sciences and philosophy and other educational sectors rather than just musicians. At UCSB I entered into a performance program much like the program I had taken part in at New England Conservatory. Immediately after my entrance I was selected to play in the Honors Scholarship Woodwind Quintet. I filled my days with various educational studies, in addition to music performance and was soon heavily engrossed in preparing for the various music competitions available at the university. At the same time, my mental disorder continued to develop its own personal partitioning of my mind; leaving me with even less room for reality and making more room for the delusions that were to come. However, my career was still progressing well as I was becoming more well known as a musician.

Over the next six months, my bouts of depression worsened and the panic attacks increased in number and severity. With each successive panic attack, I dreaded the act of making music more and more. Concerts became a hellish ordeal. Although performing on stage had never been a problem for me in the past, it now presented a serious barrier to the future of my career. I had always relished the idea of sharing my music with an audience. It was the ultimate compliment to have an audience to play for. However, the combination of panic attacks and depression had taken that unbridled joy away from me, and replaced the warm response in my stomach that I always felt during a performance, with bitter cold dread.

After a year filled with exhausting performances and the anguish of a degrading mind, I fell into a bizarre personal period of expressionism. In this new period, all I would wear was black. It suited my mood and made dressing simple although it was monotonous. I felt anesthetized most of the time and even tears would not come anymore. In the meantime, I found a large number of opportunities for performance in this much larger university and began auditioning for the various competitions which were available to me. I auditioned for and won the concerto competition three years in a row. I also won a concerto competition along with my sister playing the Mozart Flute and Harp Concerto. I won three Music Affiliate Scholarship Awards for excellence in music performance and at 21, I premiered my brother's piece Silver

Wind and performed the piece in Lotte Lehman Hall before a sold out theater.

My grandparent's, who normally attended my performances, were determined to be present at the world premiere of my brother's piece for solo flute and synthesizer. My grandfather was especially excited to hear this piece, as he was just recovering from a failed throat operation whose source was a deep cancer and he hoped to hear me perform one last time. Late in my grandfather's life, he developed cancer of the larynx and because he was hoarse normally when he spoke, due to heavy smoking, the doctor's did not determine the seriousness of his condition until he began to choke and could not easily swallow. Upon further examination his doctor determined that the hoarseness was due to a malignancy wrapped around his vocal chords. His doctors determined that his larynx should be operated on and during the operation his larynx was removed along with his complete voice box. This left him in a silence which did not fit well for such a strong man, who was accustomed to using the power of his voice and its prosody to emphasize serious points and influence his listeners. Grandfather's voice was as much a part of his persona and being as his physique and physical presence. He was a person lost after his operation. He acquired a synthetic voice microphone and attempted to converse using this difficult and clumsy instrument.

It was while he was using this instrument, which he eventually gave up, that he came to hear this particular performance. I was pleased that he had made the effort to come and was excited to do my best to send my love across the audience, to this man who had been so special to me. After the concert, I came out into the audience and he was beaming with admiration for his granddaughter's performance. I could tell he was uncomfortable with his situation but he continued to speak briefly with his new speaking apparatus and hugged me tightly to show his approval of my playing. This meant more to me than any of the applause that I had become used to in my performance career and I treasure it to this day. It was only a short few days later that I learned that they had found additional cancer cells in his lungs and that he had very little time left to live.

I earned my performance awards through great practice and sacrifice, living with the torment of my mind and yet maintaining the discipline to perform. I realized that I must develop the perseverance and character which had been so strongly imbued in my mind through the lessons taught to me in my youth. I understood, in a small way, the bravery and character that my grandfather demonstrated, as he lived out the rest of his life in silence, having lost an important piece of his self–image and accepted his death with grace and dignity. I only saw him twice after that night and I tried to keep in my memory, not the image of him as he became more and more ill, but the image of him as a younger man, throwing me in the air and returning me to the safety of his arms with a proud smile covering his face.

As my performance successes continued to grow, my difficulties with my mental disorder continued to increase. One night, after a particularly difficult symphonic performance, I felt the full pressures of my depression and growing hallucinations. I contemplated once more, the alternatives between a tormented life and the release that death could bring. I sat very quietly in my room, alone except for the company of panic and depression and cut my forearm slowly with a razor blade. I was not trying to kill myself. I just needed to feel like I was still among the living. I wanted to feel pain, because pain was honest and was a real feeling of existence. While not the most pleasant of sensations, it did show to me that I still exist. I don't really remember what prompted me to cut myself, but I do remember that I had been working on some home crafts on a card table in my room for the local county fair and was using a razor blade to cut some rather stiff cardboard, making access to the cutting tool very easy. The night I cut myself for the very first time, I was actually rather calm. I slowly picked up the razor and went over to my bed and softly, almost caressingly, ran the blade over my arm. I then started using more and more pressure, until the blade left a bloody trail upon the surface of my skin. I thought that it would hurt more, but instead the pain was minimal, at least in my altered state of consciousness. I sat very still, watching the blood ooze slowly from the long cuts I had made. Watching these cuts bleed, somehow gave me a twisted sense of accomplishment. In my unreality, I felt more alive and tension free than I had before. These after effects brought upon by a brain that was sick, and the result of a growing mental disorder, caused me to cut myself again and again. Whenever things seemed overwhelming, I cut myself again and within the mantle of my depression and my ever–growing disorder, it made me feel better. I had to take great pains to cover my arms and hide the cuts from my family but they soon noticed the cuts anyway. I made up weak excuses like, the cat scratched me or I scraped my arm on the door. Needless to say, I did not fool them for very long; after a few weeks there were simply too many cuts on both of my arms to conceal their source. At one point I had over fifty cuts in various stages of healing. I had no intention of stopping. My illness had brought me to the point that mutilating my body seemed to help me to cope with my degrading mental state and soon became a part of my sick daily routine. It would take years and expert help to find a better way to deal with my problems, but before I would do that, I would suffer more severely from the growing depression and delusions that were destroying my mind. Even after much help, there were still times that my distorted mind would cause me to revert back to the blade.

This mental illness would have its moments of comic relief. In addition to the depression and delusions, it inserted in my mind a mania which would change my personality and take me on roller coaster rides between total elation and complete depression. One day, late in my junior year, I woke up with my mind's new gift, complete mania and it single–handedly lifted the shroud of depression that had covered my mind for so long. In its place were racing, leaping, thoughts. My mind seemed very full, all of a sudden, crowded with dangerous intervallic leaps of thought very much like Domenico Scarlatti's Cat's Fugue, with its theme of wide and irregular skips in ascending motion; like a cat walking helter skelter across the length of a piano keyboard. I felt the elation that only this illness can bring. Despite the strange tritones that were bouncing around within my mind, I liked the energetic feeling it gave me. For the first time in months of depression, I was happy and filled with energy. That morning, in my manic state, I got up and after wearing funereal garb to the university for over two years, I chose to wear a bright red pantsuit. I did not know until much later that the wild staccato of thoughts in my head were due to one of the symptoms of Schizoaffective Disorder. I went to school ecstatically happy and practically skipped into rehearsals. The panic attacks had vanished into thin air and the depression had left with them. I certainly was not going to tempt fate by sending out a search party. I laughed unprompted, at the most inane things that my friends would say and all those who knew me felt I had achieved some form of metamorphosis. I was once again fun to be around and my sense of humor seemed heightened.

However, the roller coaster ride took a dip and the feelings of happiness left as quickly as they had come. Within a two-week period, my life abruptly decelerated back to a very depressing and painfully slow funeral dirge. The depression seemed ten times worse coming after the extreme highs of my episode of mania. It is the ultimate cruelty, that this mental disorder will bring you happiness briefly so that you can better contrast the true happiness that you have lost with the deep depression and torturous delusions that you must live with. It is much like the techniques used by the medieval torturer, who once he had you upon the rack, would ease the stretching of your muscles so that he could convince you he really was your friend and could make sure that you would not become inured to the unending pain of torture. I could not get out of bed in the morning and I suffered from terrible periods of sleeplessness. The lack of sleep brought on even more cutting. I would have failed school if members of my family had not come in everyday and coaxed me out of bed; pushed me into the shower; and made sure that I was off to class on time. I would float listlessly through the day staring off into space in class after class. I thought more and more about leaving school and giving in to the devastation that was my mind.

At my lowest moment something wonderful happened that did not depend on my music or the playing of my flute. I had always depended on my music to fulfill the great gnawing need I had for emotional fulfillment and yet little by little this disease of mine cruelly diminished the love I received through the making of music. I was soon to find that there were other kinds of loves to be had and this was the beginning of the exciting world of physical love.

As I lie here in the darkness of my hospital room, remembering earlier times, I wonder how much of my love for the flute comes from my body or from that organ in the brain we call the amygdala. I wonder how close, after all, producing the sounds of my flute and passing them over the heads of a rapt audience uses those very same nerve endings, sensors and body functions that also makes physical love so exciting and magic. In the end, when we touch someone else's skin, or feel the delicate softness of a rose petal, we put into play much of our body's response to life itself. Whether it's passing air over a flute's embouchure plate, or gently grasping the hand of someone you love, is it not the same neurons playing in concert their great symphony of interaction that gives us the ability to experience this special experience? Is love the same, whether its medium is the undulation of air carrying the sounds of music, or the gentle tactile pressures produced by loving fingers moving gently over our bodies? All of this about love and communication has been well recorded in the books of philosophers and artists over the millennia, but it is still left to the special reality each of us owns, for us to construct this combination of subjective and emotional reality for ourselves and to then combine it with the objective rhythm of life's cadence. No matter how many ways we are introduced to love, and no matter how many ways the wise philosophers speak of it, it is a new experience for each of us, with feelings individual to our own bodies and our own minds. As much as we generalize with words, physical love is special and different for each of us. My love, or at least my memory of it, begins with the first time I met Allan as an adult towards the end of my junior year at UCSB. I was very active at the time in concert performances, not only at the university, but at many other theaters off campus. It was one of these off campus performances that led to my chance meeting with Allan.

I stood at the counter of Carl's Jr. fidgeting with the familiar nervousness I felt before every performance. I had learned to ignore the stares from other people as they looked at me, a woman dressed in a floor length, midnight–black taffeta gown in the middle of the afternoon. I guess I did look a bit out of place dressed in what could easily be taken for funereal garb, calmly ordering a diet soda and an order of fries. Over the years as a classical musician I have gotten used to the looks of pity from people whenever I go out to a store or restaurant in concert dress. Their first reaction is to assume I have just come from or am just going to a funeral. I have received numerous condolences in my career, from well meaning but misguided individuals. As usual I was in a rush trying to get to a matinee performance of Beethoven's 9th symphony and had spent all morning rehearsing. There had been no time for sustenance, so I raced to the nearest fast food restaurant to get a bite to eat so I could get through the long performance ahead. As I stood in line, waiting for my fries and coke, I heard a familiar voice out of my past calling my name. This voice would change my life forever. I spun around and found myself face to face with a warm, friendly smile behind a big bushy moustache—It took a second to recognize that this was my good friend and chorus partner from my high school years. I had not seen Allan for many years, and his name did not immediately come to mind. He looked at me quizzically—"Don't you remember me"? I struggled to recall his name and just when I was about to embarrass myself and admit I knew the face but not the name, I blurted out, "Of course I remember you, Allan" and he smiled that great beaming smile that he would get whenever I said something that pleased him. Allan immediately asked if had I been to a funeral. I laughed out loud, an inside joke we would come to appreciate together in the months to come. "No, I said. I am about to play in a concert at the Lobero Theater." Just then my order was thrust into my hands and I quickly turned to find a table. I only had a few minutes, until orchestra Call. Allan asked me quietly, if he could join me. I said I would enjoy the company; we could catch up on old times. I sat down feeling surprisingly self-conscious and looked across the table at this friend from my past. I thought to myself, what a handsome man he had grown into. He was tall and broad shouldered and his face was dark and handsome but still retained that gentleness and sensitivity that I remembered in that shy, skinny boy I knew all those years ago. I remember he had been a hesitant young boy and now he seemed so self-assured and at ease with himself. What a pair we made, anyone else waiting in line for a hamburger, who looked in our direction, would see two smiling, happy people, one dressed for a funeral and the other dressed for a casual day on the beach. Only the constant looks between us hinted at an attraction deeper than a chance meeting at a fast food restaurant. As we munched on fries, we talked about what we had been doing since our teenage years. We laughed about the hours we had spent together working on those spring musicals. I noticed that the corners of his mouth turned up, ever so slightly in a constant grin, making his face seem happy no matter what the subject. I could not believe how lucky I was to have run into Allan. I found my attraction to him deep and immediate. I looked forward to holding myself close against his body and gently touching his lips to mine. I wanted more than anything at this point to slide over to the other side of this table and feel his sensitive embrace.

Allan interrupted my secret thoughts with the words, "I was decidedly tone deaf, wasn't I?" referring to those school musicals we had performed in together. I silently agreed with his comment about tone deafness, while I assured him that it was not as bad as he remembered. In high school, Allan loved to perform and amazingly, despite his aural handicap, was cast repeatedly in the chorus. Allan would often ask me to help him with his part—and we would play "find that pitch" together, with me plunking out notes on the piano, as he meandered hopelessly around the pitch. He never really found its center, though I patiently gave him the thumbs up sign as the signal for him to raise the pitch and the thumbs down sign to lower the pitch and an emphatic O.K. sign when he finally found it. During the course of our conversation I noticed that Allan was staring at me. His eyes projected an affection that one only sees in true love. I could not help but return his stare, trying to embrace him with my arms and my eyes. I blushed as he asked me to join him for dinner later in the week. I was thrilled he had asked. I could feel the strength of the attraction between us and we eagerly made arrangements to get together the following Friday. He stepped tentatively closer to me as we started to part and gave me an unexpected gentle kiss on my cheek. His lips were soft and I looked forward to giving him a fuller kiss when we met again. As I got back into my car and drove to the Lobero theater, I began planning what I would wear on our date Friday. I felt more alive than I had felt in a long time and I was flushed with excitement about what the future held for Allan and I. I had not expected to find the love of my life over a coke and fries. My dreams were filled that night with a different kind of music.

Over the ensuing months, Allan turned out to be one of the most sensitive, funny, loving and romantic men I had ever met. I looked forward to each new meeting in that he would quickly pull me towards him and kiss me in a long, passionate touching of lips, as though he had just returned from a long separation. I looked forward to those kisses and the comfort they gave me when we were apart. Allan had a special flare for the romantic that was both passionate and lively. He often combined it with a broad sensitivity I had come to expect from this gentle man. On our first Valentine's Day together he had stuffed cards and hundreds of pieces of tiny confetti through the narrow slits in my locker at the university and attached helium balloons to my locker handle. As I looked at this wonderful and sensitive Valentine surprise, I marveled at the fact that this wonderful man had reentered my life. He even stuffed an entire bagel with cream cheese, (my favorite food), into my tiny music department mailbox for me to "discover". It was hardly a difficult find since the bagel bulged out of the tiny compartment causing the cream cheese to flow down over the assorted mail below. Just as I felt he could not improve on this day's play of romantic fervor, he showed up after my last class in a tuxedo that melted my heart on the spot. As he took me in his arms and I leaned against his chest, I felt the warmth of his safe, strong arms and I wished that this feeling of completeness would last beyond this brief moment and live in my waking consciousness as a shield against the dark world of my disordered mind.

Allan was extremely supportive of my music career, attending every concert I played and at times making a fool of himself, leaping to his feet at the end of each work, whistling and cheering for me regardless of whether I was the soloist or just a member of the orchestra.

Allan allowed me to forget for a while about my problems, and sometimes even laugh at them. He loved me unconditionally and seemed to understand all of my little idiosyncrasies. He held my hand when I would get nervous before a performance, gently whispering in my ear how beautiful and talented I was and how lucky he was to have me; but I felt like I was cheating him, because I had not yet told him my biggest secret. I was afraid his feelings towards me might change if he knew that I had a brain disorder. Would he understand the bouts of depression, panic attacks and hallucinations? Would I lose him if I were up front with him about my mental illness? The question haunted me daily, but mercifully one night the worry and guilt was put to rest.

Allan asked me out to a very romantic dinner to celebrate the sixth month anniversary of our first chance meeting and the fact that I was now a college senior. After that wonderful dinner, Allan asked if we could "Go somewhere and talk." I pictured an evening filled with hugs and passionate embraces. When we finally arrived at our favorite spot near the beach, he turned to me and with a seriousness I had not seen before said, "I must tell you something very important". The gentle curl that was always on his lips, had left and its absence created a face I did not recognize. I instantly thought of myself as the problem. I could not conceive that he was about to confess something to me that was his secret alone. I instantly filled with panic, my mind was screaming silently, "He knows my secret and I have lost the love of my life."

It was a chilly night and it did not take long for the windows to completely fog up which added to my feeling of suffocating panic about what Allan must tell me. I had that same awful feeling in the pit of my stomach that I got when I played a wrong note in concert, a note you can never take back, a performance kept from perfection forever due to a careless error. My performance on the stage of life had already been marred by mental illness and now all the wrong notes I had played through the years, were going to destroy the one good thing I had found in my life outside of music. Allan began to speak quietly and hesitatingly, "I have something to tell you about myself". I was so relieved that he did not want to talk about me, that I could hardly hear what followed. He wanted to be honest, "completely honest" with me and therefore he wanted to share with me what he considered to be his biggest secret. I was dumbfounded; Allan had a secret too? The rest of the conversation consisted of Allan baring his soul to me and my anxiety grew with the realization that in all likelihood I would be expected to do the same. I did not listen carefully enough to Allan's words. I was only considering my requirement to confess to him. I missed most of what he said, and the rest of his comments were drowned out by the rush of panic enveloping my mind. I sat there, staring into his eyes, smiling weakly, trying to listen to his "secrets" but not hearing anything but my mind's inner voices. Having missed most of what Allan had to say, was a fact that would come back to haunt me in ways I could never have envisioned. Soon it was my turn to "share". I took a deep breath and told him everything. My "secrets" poured out of me so fast, my tongue could hardly keep up with my mind's thoughts. I hardly took a breath between sentences, recounting my problems with panic and depression. After I finished my mini-speech, I fell silent; out of breath; staring into his eyes, searching for the tiniest indication of how he felt about all of this new information. I flinched slightly, as Allan unexpectedly took my hands in his and said in his most sincere, compassionate voice, that none of my problems changed the way he felt about me. We kissed a long passionate, knowing kiss between two people who no longer maintained a barrier of secrets between them. The emotion welled up in my throat and he held me while I cried tears of happiness and relief. We had both bared our souls, walking through the fires of painful honesty and emerged from them a stronger couple, a more complete couple. I thought to myself, now nothing could ever come between us. I was wrong.

As the months progressed into a year I was completely content. When Allan and I weren't together, we were on the phone talking about every possible aspect of life, its problems and our future together. Our phone conversations lasted for hours and occurred almost every night. Each night that I would get a call, we would spend hours talking about our loves, hopes, disappointment and triumphs. Neither one of us wanted the conversation to end and we acted like teenagers when it came time to say goodnight and hang up the phone.

I thought that my life was finally taking a turn for the better. My music career was back on track; I had won four competitions the first year I was with Allan and it all seemed too good to be true. Allan continued to be extremely attentive. When I got sick he would bring meals to my house and sit with me and give me the comfort that I needed. Allan was so sensitive, so funny, I was sure at last that nothing could ever ruin what we had. We began talking seriously about marriage and children and the future we would have together after we were married. I felt like God was finally making amends for the suffering I had endured over the past several years, but it was not to be.

Shortly after the first anniversary of our first meeting, he called and said that he needed to see me right away. His voice was serious once again and reminded me of our earlier discussion in his car that difficult night. He sounded unsure of himself and uneasy during the entire phone conversation. Alarms started going off in my mind. I agreed to meet with him at the university outside of the music library. I was disturbed by the fact that he could not give me this important message over the phone; after all, we no longer had secrets between us. But he refused to say more, stating that what he had to say, he needed to tell me in person. My every instinct cried out to me that this conversation might end our relationship. I stood shaking outside the library, anxiously waiting for Allan to arrive; my mind spinning with the thoughts of possibilities yet defined.

Allan arrived at our meeting and we both slowly sat down on the long, cold tile planter, outside the music library. Even though we sat in the brightness of the noon sun, I felt the darkness of midnight and the cold of unfulfilled wishes. He seemed extremely nervous and we made small talk for a few minutes. There were many long, uncomfortable silences; it seemed neither of one of us wanted to talk as we had so fervently in the past. I finally broke the steady stream of small talk by speaking in the calmest voice I could manage, and asked him to tell me why he needed to see me face to face. What was it that was so very important that he had to tell me in person? My voice began to shake along with my body as I repeated my question. I wished that perhaps we could freeze time so that I would never have to hear the stinging words that emptied my soul and destroyed my dreams of true love.

He cleared his throat, as he always did when he was nervous, and slowly and quietly began to talk to me about the fact that he could not marry me, because he had serious issues with his sexual orientation and was confused by his actions. I sat stunned as he relayed a long and twisted tale of his life–long struggle to find his true sexual identity—My mind flashed back to that conversation at the beach—the "secrets" he had shared—the story about being found in bed with another man by his father during a Christmas break from college. Allan was trying to tell me that he may have been a homosexual as long ago as high school. I was at a loss for words when he asked me what I thought about his "news". I felt the numbness of someone in deep shock. I did not know what he wanted me to say in response. I felt tears welling in my eyes. I loved him. I wanted to marry him and have his children. Now that was never going to happen. I fought back the flowing tears, as the images of a future with Allan faded into memories never born. I sobbed, "Its over, I'm so sorry for both of us". If it could only have been… "Allan, you are the love of my life." To my disbelief, he quietly said, "I still really want to see you, I love you". He told me then, that he was sure that his feelings for other men would eventually disappear and ultimately we would be able to live our lives together. Without thinking, I stated what was in my heart at that moment; that I could not risk marrying him and then find out two years into the marriage that he was going to leave me for another man. I could not live with that kind of separation. I loved him deeply, but it was clear that we had no future together. It was over. I broke down and ran to my car and sobbed for hours until my back ached and my stomach hurt. The entire situation seemed surreal. Was I dreaming? How could he have let me believe that we had a future together, when all along he knew he had feelings for men? How could I have deceived myself so completely? It took days for me to tell my family what had happened and I sank into one of the worst depressions of my life. I still have not recovered from the loss of my one great love. It was with Allan that I could feel the true depths of my emotions and I will never forget that.

Two months later, I graduated from UCSB with high honors. I took with me my Fouregere, my diploma and my memories of a love lost.

I lie very still in my hospital bed with my eyes shut, feeling the remains of those memories. I can feel the weight of my body sinking ever deeper into the bed's blankets. I breathe very quietly now, trying to remember one more time his gentle touch, holding me in his arms and the sweet warmth of love as complete as I could conjure with my beloved flute. The telling of life's frames usually leaves out those events that cause changes in our lives, but in the recall of this frame, I know full well the depth to which my life was changed by this encounter with Allan's physical love. My brain lets me contemplate with what seems to be true reality; the movements of our intertwining and the many sensual feelings that I had for this other human being. It seems so different now that I recall it, but it is much like the memory of a performance well done but lacking the proper ending. There is no applause from the audience and all is still as the theater lights dim into blackness.

3

The Angry Soprano

※

The Dissonant Opera of my Psychosis

I slowly turn over quietly and fall into a deep troubled sleep. In the morning, I hear the rapid knock of the nurse who sticks her head through the door and asks me how I feel. In the daylight, the room appears much less empty and it is filled with the play of light off of corners and shadows artfully placed by images passing through the window at the side of my bed. My stay in this hospital has given me the chance to think quietly about myself, and the life I have led. It has given my mind a much needed calm, within which to recall the actions of my youth that have taken me to this place. Only now can I begin to feel some hope for my ability to fight this disorder and return to my life of music. The memories become less traumatic as the days pass and I return to music performance. The remembrances here have been almost as vivid as when they were lived. In some ways these memories have replaced my life itself. My life has clearly contained many happy moments, mixed with the sorrow brought about by my mental illness, but it has been good to see my life once again in the quiet of this room, and to better understand those events that helped me to arrive at this difficult point. It has been said that memories are ephemeral, difficult to catch and keep fresh in your mind, but here in the darkness of my room, it has been as though I had attended a private viewing of my life, complete with its emotions, my music and my love. It has helped me to understand those places in my life in which my path has been filled with ruts and cobblestones, forcing me to change directions many times, but it has never changed my long-term goals; to make music and communicate my love to others through the sounds I create. I feel stronger having had these experiences and am more resolute than ever to begin my life again, having within me a certainty that somehow I will find the answers that I need. Those important memories begin to dim next to the growing brightness of my future plans. I think I am ready to play music again. I feel more positive about myself than I have in many months. I know that staying in this room will not give me the chance to act out those plans I have had so long in the making. I feel that it is time to leave the hospital and return to my music and my life. I feel I need to end this stay, which seems like a lifetime, even though I have been here less than three weeks. But there is still one remembrance that stays vivid in my mind and that is the tragedy of my relationship with Allan. Even after I leave the hospital and return home, I will find that the emptiness left by the loss of my love for Allan, remains with me.

It has been only four months since my graduation from the university; four months since the tragic separation from Allan. Before I had entered the hospital, I had spent much of my time in deep depression while fighting the ever-growing need to escape my mind's bizarre delusions. It was difficult for me to play my flute and I lacked the desire to practice with the regularity needed to keep the flute a part of myself. I essentially separated from the instrument of my music; just as I had separated from Allan but now it is time for me to take up my flute once more and to pour those emotions which were directed at my lost love, into my music once again.

Even as I begin to practice again, my days still are filled with a longing for Allan. The days follow one another with a mechanical sameness. I long for change in my life. I try to regain the enthusiasm that had welled up within me just before I left the hospital. In the midst of my melancholy, I receive a call from a conductor who I have always admired; a well-known conductor I will call Maestro Sanduval. He had a long series of triumphs in Europe and in the U.S. and I was anxious to perform under his baton. After asking about my health, he asks me if I would perform the Mozart Concerto in D Major for Flute and Orchestra. My heart jumps as he says those words. I find myself saying yes to the maestro with the same fervor I would have said yes to marriage vows. I accept the maestro's offer and my body begins to feel alive again. At least for the moment, I forget the disarray of my present life and begin to think about the joy of making music. I have played this masterpiece before, but now I feel I must bring it to even higher standards of perfection. This performance needs to fill the emptiness left by Allan. It needs to substitute for the fragments of my life that had been taken away from me by my mental disorder. This performance needs to refill my being with the joy of life once again.

It has been so long since I have picked up my flute in a serious attempt to make music, that I am somewhat timid as I begin my first private rehearsal of the Mozart.

I begin this journey to a performance by playing simple exercises, at one–quarter tempo, until my fingers are flying through the standard scales and arpeggios. I sigh briefly and opening Mozart's score, I begin to hear this classical masterpiece within my mind. I slowly hear its beautiful melodic lines and rich harmonic texture. I hear the entrance of the strings that fill my measures of rest and I prepare for my entrance. I lift the flute to my mouth. In the quiet of my practice studio I hear in my mind, the intricate weaving of complex modulations between the high winds and the strings. I imagine the conductor, baton raised, ready to cue my entrance. I take a deep breath in anticipation of the challenging and technically difficult passages before me and I begin to play. I become lost in the music as my fingers move quickly over the keys of my flute. After two hours of this intense concentration, I stop for a brief period, still hearing the sounds of the orchestra in my head; I sit back in my chair and quietly enjoy the calm of this brief respite in my private rehearsal.

My mind returns briefly to those long sweet kisses that I would no longer have and I try to fill the silence with further thoughts of Mozart. I finger over my flute briefly and silently follow the notes on the great manuscript before me, not using the mouthpiece of my flute, but merely the quiet music within my mind to fill the parts written by that young composer, written at twenty–three, an age very close to mine. It was said that within Mozart's mind, he could create a great symphonic hall, which he could fill with his own personal music; where he could define each note, chord and phrase as though he were there in that hall conducting the aural images in front of his own symphony orchestra. Writing the music within the silence of his mind, Mozart was both the conductor and the audience. Later, the great master would record the symphony for others to play as though an act of afterthought by putting quill to paper and placing the blackness of the notes on the page, just so, as in remembrance of some great performance he was privileged to hear. I ponder the genius of such creativity; was this the greatest use of his mind? Where I struggled to keep out the unwanted intrusions of another reality, Mozart's mind was left clear and open, so that the music could fill every space within his own personal hall.

I continue to ponder the level of such genius. Picking up my flute thoughtfully, and fingering it briefly, I begin to play once again, the magnificent notes of Mozart's great Flute Concerto in D. I fill my head with the sounds of the orchestra as it accompanies my flute. Slowly, I become aware of an added sound; clearly not the sound of the orchestra in my head or my flute. It is a sound like no other I have heard before. A loud, coarse voice, like an aged operatic soprano reaching for a note well beyond her range. The horrifying sound rings through my head, emptying my mind of all other thoughts, leaving this new voice with an acoustic chamber in which its terrifying message echoes unendingly. This new voice takes over the sound of the orchestra; it muffles the sound of my flute. The sound clashes eerily against the melodic line. The sound echoes back and forth across the now empty space of my mind with nothing to slow it down or to mute its sharp intensity. It is unlike any human voice; it has a rasping shrillness and a hard-edged quality that takes it beyond human experience. I am terrified. I stand in my studio, still with fear; my mind in confusion; my flute held dangling at my side like an appendage that has been broken off at the joint. Where is the noise coming from? I can feel my pulse pounding in my temples, as the tone rapidly becomes unbearably loud. The voice seems to be reaching for a High C, which turns quickly into a hoarse scream; high in pitch with guttural undertones. I struggle to make sense of the noise I am hearing. I run to my studio door and out into the hallway, searching for the source of the piercing voice that never seems to need a breath. I run into the kitchen and stand awestruck by the sight of a surreal scene; my sister in-law standing calmly at the kitchen stove, slowly stirring noodles in a large pot, her motions measured and relaxed, as she slowly pours some milk, seemingly deaf to the cacophony of sound slicing through the room and bouncing off the walls. I am incredulous. How can she be so calm? Doesn't she hear the woman's screams? Doesn't she find the knife-like pitches as deafening as I do? I notice that the screaming is as intense in the kitchen as it is in my studio. Panicked and confused, I run to my bedroom and quickly open a window. Perhaps the noise is emanating from outside the house? I crawl up on my bed and jam my ear up against the window screen, so closely that I can smell its musty odor. But the screaming is neither louder nor softer. It is in this horrible moment, that I realize that the voice I am hearing is **only** in my head. I stand in dumbfounded silence, for how long I am not sure, and yet the sound is still strong within my brain. This ungodly voice is giving a contorted, private concert, just for me. Then, as abruptly as it started, the screaming stops. The silence is as unnerving as when the screaming had begun. But my relief is intense. The angry voice has mercifully concluded its performance.

  The abrupt introduction of this voice into my life was brief, not even a full minute, but my life was forever altered by that loud disorganized sound. I would come to call this sound The Angry Soprano. I had no idea at the time that the angry soprano would return for encore after encore, and as my disorder worsened, bring other horrors with her.

As a concert flutist I have listened to and performed with some wonderful musicians; sopranos whose voices melted in my ears like the soft, melodic sounds of a faun awakening in the afternoon. I have always loved operatic singing. To me the angry soprano was an ironic twist. My brain chose something that I loved deeply and warped it into something ugly and disorienting.

I call her the angry soprano, but she is not worthy of the name, in that she possesses neither the lilting voice of a soprano nor the lyrical sounds of such a voice in concert. Her voice is far too shrill and she is far too angry to maintain the fine qualities of music, well performed. She has come to invade my inner spaces as an unwelcome occupant, as though she were an uninvited guest, living with me in my house and callously commenting on all aspects of my life, my opinions, my love, and the very views I have of existence and death. She is worse than my worst enemy, in that I must live with her everywhere that I go. She can enter at will, any conversation I have. She can and does disrupt my music. She shares my bed and the very intimate dreams that should be left to me alone. She is even there during my bath and during my natural functions in the bathroom. She is there when I eat. She is there when I am happy. She is there when I am angry. She is always there. Living with another human being is an experience that all of us have at one time or another; it may be our parent, it may be a loved one, but it is the worst type of coupling to live with someone whom you despise and who wants only the worst for you in such an intimate and complete way. You can never escape; or find a place in your room, or those spaces in your mind where this person cannot enter. Yes, I call her the angry soprano, but the names I really have for her are far more heinous than I use for my worst enemies. I do not respect this person and I know I must fight with all of my will power, to erase her from my existence.

I have thought much since the angry soprano has begun to reside with me and within me, about the complexities of existence and the rich qualities that life has to offer. But even the beauty of clouds against a blue sky, or the transient colors of a rich sunset, can no longer be enjoyed in solitary peace. My thoughts and my emotions are forced into the background by the vicious comments of this unwanted guest. All of us have times when we would like to merge into the world of conversations around us and lie quietly, contemplating the day's events or think about the complexities of life on earth. I can no longer do that. I am free to leave my parents, or their guests, or my brother, or my sister and retire to my room, but I must have this one vulgar, stupid, aggressive, disgusting, overbearing, insensitive and unwanted guest with me. I can no longer receive even a moment of peace, or the time in which to re-gather my thoughts about those plans or actions which are important to my life and which cause me concern. I must constantly share the inanities, epithets and just plain incomprehensible, pre-symbolic language that this unwanted guest uses. She is slowly crowding out of my mind, all of my hopes and dreams and worst of all, the love that I have for life itself.

So, I call her the Angry Soprano, but it gives her far more dignity than she will ever deserve and gives to her soulless entity, sensitivity to life, which she does not possess. I am sure that she is a creation directly from hell and has been sent to me to ensure that my life has less meaning than it deserves. My hope is that if I fight this hard enough, I will someday be able to evict her from my mind and find the peace that I once had and the privacy to contemplate my own thoughts as I wish.

I speak of the angry soprano with words that I love, such as "aria" and "concert", in order to smooth the edges of her inhuman viciousness. The inner horrors she has created for me through her rantings and epithets, are beyond the realm of my feelings for life, and so I talk about arias and concerts, so that I will not relive the horrors she presents to me, as I try to think or speak about her presence. I realize that the words I use are filled with the lyricism and harmony and depth of meaning that are part of great music, but they make the telling of her terrible deeds, as she tries to destroy my very existence, more bearable. The angry soprano shattered any notion I ever had about mercy and new beginnings.

After the initial episode, I prayed that I would never have to endure anything like that again, and I tried to attribute it to exhaustion. I was definitely not getting enough sleep and I thought perhaps that was the problem.

I spend more and more of my nights in the darkness of my room, with only the illumination of my small clock to comfort me with the passing of time. I need desperately to talk to someone and share the hopelessness of my situation, but my only companion now is my flute lying silent in my lap. I pick up my flute and finger it softly and begin to play quietly *The Afternoon Of A Faun* by Claude Debussy, which I will soon be playing in concert. The sweet undulating sounds of the flute, implying the awakening of a young deer in Debussy's forest, gives me a calmness that I rarely enjoy in these days of the angry soprano. The darkness itself becomes a salve to my troubled mind. I try to lose myself within the peace of this black setting.

The darkness invades my mind and yet it is soft–shouldered, letting my thoughts flow slowly and softly out into the room. I hear the gentle roll of a rocker, as it moves slowly back and forth, taking my mind to other places. I keep wondering about my mind. I know it's somewhere in the catacombs of my brain looking for the comfort of thoughts long past. "You know", I say aloud, "I miss conversations we have had more than you know", and I hear the rocker move more quickly. He's more quiet tonight than usual, maybe he is also thinking thoughts tied loosely to his brain, waiting for a mindful resolution that sits well within his body in the darkness.

I don't mind the silent spaces; the quiet connects us more strongly than our touch. After all, he is my grandfather, and I love to feel his words flow over me like gentle reassuring fingers. When I was smaller, he would pick me up with those strong hands and hold me over his head and throw me into the air while I squirmed with delight, knowing full well he would catch me before I hit the ground. I reminisce aloud to him about doing this and he rocks again with added speed, the rhythm of the chair becomes a soft accompaniment to this dark conversation. He was a self–made man, whom I loved very much for his innate toughness of spirit and the straight mental paths he constructed for my young mind to follow.

I looked up to him my whole life. He gave meaning to the musical term sforzando (strong accent). His whole body was one giant gesture of welcome strength. He was a presence that gave my life structure and safety. I think about his image as I see him in the chair, slowly rocking back and forth, in the velvet black of my silent reverie. But, everything changes and to remind me of that, the moon interrupts our conversation with its fine narrow arms of light, lighting only a part of my room with the timid touch of a stranger interrupting a private conversation. Its glowing fingers slide gently across my grandfather's face as he rocks in and out of the interrupted moonlight.

I remember when I was six years old getting caught picking a pomegranate, after he told me specifically not to, in that forceful voice that he used to sway opinions and influence actions. I love pomegranates; the smell, the little seeds that burst in your mouth delivering tiny deliciously sweet red dreams to your tongue. I didn't think that I would get caught, so I took a chance and sneaked into the back yard to find a special pomegranate. My grandfather, seemingly able to see everywhere, came charging in my direction, and using his most ominous voice, warned me off as though I were the snake interrupting the lovers of Eden. Of course, I was no match for his size and with a vice like grip; his hand went around my entire arm, lifting me off the ground until he could decide the proper punishment. I apologized profusely, but nothing would stop him. My punishment required raking leaves from arguably the biggest sycamore tree in the county, which just happened to reside in their large front yard. Needless to say, I never picked pomegranates off that tree again without grandpa's permission.

My mind comes back to the flute lying in my hands. I had been practicing in the dark when these meanderings started. "I need to practice a bit more," I said softly to the figure rocking in the chair. Grandpa always liked to hear me play.

The room had become lighter, as the moon raised itself toward the high roundness of the night sky. I could see Grandpa's face more clearly in the edges of the light. His eyes still had the same squinty strength that I was accustomed to, but the rest of his face seemed distorted and strange. I put down my flute and looked more closely at him. The skin hung down strangely from his face, in broad ribbons of flesh, separated so that you could see the underlying bones of his cheeks. He appeared dead. That's right I thought, gasping audibly. He is dead. Funny, I thought, there's no smell. But he is here with me—now—in my room. "I have missed you Grandpa. I've missed you a lot." He did not speak, but beckoned me to continue playing. I slowly pick up my flute and begin again the dark soft tones of this ode to a young faun, moving quietly in the shadowed dim light of late afternoon. My Grandfather speaks, but I cannot understand all of what he says. His voice is raspy and uneven, as though he is speaking under water. He says he likes what I am playing and I'm not sure what else. So, I continue to play this piece, written by a man who had been dead for many years, played for a man who is dead. How many people have died since this piece was written I wonder silently? How many people have listened to this music who would soon die? I look at my Grandfather once again; he is slowly rocking with his eyes shut, apparently lost in the sounds of this piece. The music fills the darkness as I play the flute softly in my bedroom, for my dead Grandfather. The music takes on a special meaning for the two of us.

My grandfather died a very painful death. He suffered with lung cancer for several years before dying in his living room in a rented hospital bed. He was always such an incredibly strong man, standing 6' 4" tall. Even as he rocked, he appeared to have survived death itself and was still a source of strength and comfort to me here in the darkness of my room.

Since I was unable to tell anyone else about my private concerts for my Grandfather, for fear that my family would believe that I had lost the last precious shreds of my sanity, I wrote a letter to myself. I thought perhaps if I placed these thoughts down on paper, they would seem less bizarre, less upsetting. I wrote...

> *How am I going to explain this (the angry soprano and my private concerts for my dead grandfather)? Can I explain this in a way that anyone would understand? People are going to think that I have finally gone completely mad. Have I? I can no longer think rationally about that question. Even as I write this note, the angry soprano is commenting, but I am trying to ignore her vicious views. I have told my doctor some of the things I have seen and heard, but he silently looks back at me without giving an answer. I understand that quizzical look; that look that other peoples faces exhibit when they think that you are completely mad. Maybe grandpa really was here; stranger things have happened. I have seen so many television programs that support the position that there are other dimensions; perhaps there really are angels and spirits that have yet to find peace for their souls. I have this uneasy feeling that you get when you look down from the top of a cliff, that anxious feeling that you get in your stomach when you see that great distance between you and the ground. I can't seem to step away from the edge. I feel like I am constantly walking on the very rim of that cliff, not safe, but not falling either. Grandpa I love you wherever you are, always know that. I wish I could put my arms around you just one more time and tell you I love you. I was so shocked by your appearance, in that first visit, that I didn't get a chance to tell you that I love you so much. I hope you can read this, I hope you are here; felt but not seen, watching over mom and me. I hope that you have found peace wherever you are, you deserve it. I love you. When I play Faun next week, you and I can*

be together again, o.k.? I don't know what I am doing here anymore, I wish I could join you grandpa, wherever you are, it can't be any worse than this, can it? I hope you like my playing next week. I am never satisfied with the way I sound anymore, but maybe you will think it is o.k. I hope so. If you see God ask Him why he is torturing me like this, whatever I need to do to appease Him I am willing to do. Please ask him Grandpa, please.

My grandfather visited me many times after our first informal concert and I learned to get used to the way he looked. After a while I no longer felt haunted, I learned to look past the specter of his face in death and tried to relate to my grandfather as if he were still alive and looking as healthy and vibrant as I remember he was. The creaking sound of the rocking chair became a comforting sound to me, rather than an overture to terror. The sound became another part of the music of my madness.

We never escape our own realities. We live with this tiny gnawing understanding that our human experience is bounded by our ability to reach out into the veridical world that we only partly know. It's the reaching out that makes our lives special, through love and friendship. Through words and sounds, through gestures and actions. That is the human condition and that is why we make love, reach for the stars and clasp hands in warm intimate conversations.

But you know, for some of us there IS one more reality. This reality does not give us comfort. It does not help us find love. It is a different kind of reality, creating our experience of experience, using nightmares and pictures of life gone awry. My reality now includes conversations with my dead grandfather and the sadistic comments of an angry soprano that resides within my head.

This voice that goes with me everywhere, I fear will follow me into the most important part of my life, the preparation of music and rehearsals in the concert hall. My worst fears were answered in the very next concerto rehearsal. I was just beginning the first movement of the Mozart Concerto, when the screaming began, only this time it seemed like more than just screaming, the angry diva was trying to say something but I couldn't make it out. Her loud voice numbed my ears to the sounds of the orchestra behind me and I inevitably lost tempo. The conductor stopped the whole orchestra and made a caustic remark about how I should be keeping my eyes on him and not the music. I could barely hear his comments through the muffling din of noise within my mind. I could see the conductor yelling something else at me from the podium, but it was like watching a silent movie. I could hear nothing over the high–pitched deafening screams. A cold, anxious panic set in; was I going to lose my ability to perform right here in front of the orchestra? I stood frozen in front of my fellow musicians, agonizing over what to do while the conductor concluded his criticisms. I was terrified. How was I going to complete the rest of the rehearsal without being able to hear the orchestra? As the inharmonious screaming in my head increased in intensity, I considered leaving the rehearsal, but that would be admitting to myself and everyone else that I was no longer capable of performing. It was now all too clear to me that performing with the angry soprano was becoming impossible.

I began to play again but the angry soprano brought home my realization of failure by attempting another duet between my flute and her hoarse, off key sounds; a duet which neither fit the music of Mozart nor the key in which it was written. I vainly attempted to continue my part of the performance. The ugly and insistent voice in my mind continued in spite of my failing performance. I could not hear the sound of my flute over the ever increasing insistence of this dominant voice. Locked in a rehearsal I could not leave, I had to play by feel and by sight. The voice continued. I relied on the warm focused air stream leaving my lips to reassure myself that I was still creating my part of the concerto. I played the rest of the Mozart with my eyes riveted to the conductor's baton, so that I would not lose tempo. I was frantically struggling to maintain the ensemble between my flute and the rest of the orchestra. I felt removed from the hall. I could see the bowing of the violins out of the corner of my eye, but I could not hear their sound. As soon as the last note of the Mozart was completed, I grabbed my music, and with tears in my eyes, hurriedly threw my flute into its case and ran from the rehearsal hall to the privacy of my car, still hearing the grossly distorted sounds of the voice in my head.

After that rehearsal, I lived in a constant state of anxiety. Each time the ugly voice started, I told myself to hang on, it <u>had</u> to be her final encore. I wished deeply that I could rid myself of this voice so that I no longer had to share my life or the same stage day after day. I hoped that she would have to leave eventually but in the depths of my mind I knew I would have to fight to destroy her dreadful presence. The thought of living with that uninvited voice on a permanent basis was too horrible to comprehend.

The angry soprano permeated everything I did. Even practicing was becoming an insurmountable chore. I couldn't play a scale without her deafening accompaniment. Countless times I tried to dissuade the angry soprano from interrupting me when I was in the middle of a practice session, but to no avail.

In spite of the presence of this angry voice during rehearsals, I managed painfully to complete each of them and leave the concert hall appearing to be in full control of myself. I was determined to play the Mozart in concert at any cost.

The night of the performance, I stand in the wings listening to the unwanted comments of the voice within my mind. I am paralyzed with fear that she will ruin this most public of my performances. The orchestra has just finished tuning and the audience is waiting silently for me to appear. In the darkness offstage, as I wait for the conductor to motion me onstage, I say a silent prayer to God to silence this voice at least for this performance; and blessedly, the angry voice becomes silent. The conductor motions for me to proceed on stage, and we walk determinedly single file to the podium. I walk in front of the conductor, concentrating only on the quiet clicking of my heels and maintaining as much as possible in my head, the sounds of the music I am about to perform. I become aware of the slight rustle of my concert dress as I walk down the isle that separates the violin sections. Still no sound from the angry soprano. I take a deep breath and make my way to center stage to the sound of welcome applause. I bow and my pulse quickens as I request an A from the oboe. The sweat is already beading on the back of my neck; and in my floor length gown the stage lights are like hot reminders of the intensity of my anguish. I look out at the audience and can just make out the tops of the heads of some of the audience members in the first few rows. I finish tuning by adjusting my flute's head joint and nod to the conductor that I am ready to begin. The conductor lifts his baton and the orchestra begins its introduction to the first movement of Mozart's Concerto in D Major. Mozart's joyous polyphony is created by the orchestra as the strings fill the hall with their warm harmonies. As I listen to these great sounds I wait quietly for my entrance. Soon the conductor cues my entrance and I begin to play. I am satisfied with the tone of my flute resonating from the back of the concert hall, entwining with the rest of the orchestra. The wretched voice is still silent. I am soon lost in the music and am reveling in the precision of technique and timing that Mozart's music commands. For a few precious measures, I forget about the voice I fear the most. The first movement is going well and a feeling of exhilaration and sheer joy envelopes my body. I begin to play a delicate passage when suddenly I hear her insulting dissonance, a concert "C" grinding against the concert "D" I am sustaining. For a moment, I am suspended within this dissonant duet. Someone in the audience coughs loudly, momentarily silencing the voice and jarring my mind back to the concerto. Back to my fingers moving smoothly up and down the keys of my flute. Back to my breathing which is now labored. The voice resumes with even more intensity. It is all I can do to hear myself over the angry soprano's screams. Her voice does not let me hear the sounds of the symphony behind me. I begin to shake with panic as the voice sings a minor second off from every note I play, creating disorientation in my mind that my music cannot overcome. With every moment of her disruptive sounds, I feel less able to continue. I desperately try to maintain my stage presence, straining as hard as I can to hear the orchestra. I keep telling myself again and again that the voice is only in my head, but the voice and I are locked in an illogical and tragic dance. The angry soprano is intent on destroying my performance; even though I am the only audience member that hears her voice, I cannot help but feel that she is projecting her powerful disruption of my music to the entire hall, and they are hearing her discordance over the beautiful music of Mozart. Her persistent voice increases in volume throughout the concerto filling my ears with loud ugly tones, obliterating the orchestra behind me. I fight for every single note in the concerto, as if my life depends on it. Each articulation, dynamic nuance and phrase requires every weapon I have in my musical arsenal. For the first time in my life I am at war with my music. This concerto will not be the ruination of my reputation. It cannot. I silently tell myself I will get through this experience, no matter how painful, no matter what the angry soprano does or says, I will play through this to the final note. I play on with all the passion left within my soul. As I play the final notes of the last movement, I can hardly see the conductor through the tears of relief that have begun to well up in my eyes. I have survived this concert in spite of the voice within my mind. I have won at least one battle with this angry soprano but I have yet to win the war. I can hardly hear the applause as the strings play their final chord and I quickly turn to the concertmaster, and shake his hand. I turn and shake the conductor's hand, almost in a moment of penance for what I have put him through, and I leave the stage. I stand backstage once more, wanting to leave the hall as soon as possible. They signal me to return to the stage for curtain calls; the applause continues. I don't want to go back out for the curtain calls while the voice still rings in my head. I cannot fully hear the applause for my performance. I wonder if the applause is for me as I bow or if it is for the conductor's interpretation or is it for the true genius who cannot be here this evening, Mozart himself. I do not know the extent of my success in this performance; the angry soprano has taken that away from me too. I want to hide in my dressing room and cry, but I continue to bow before the audience while the angry soprano throws epithets at me while telling me how poor my performance was and that I should give up the flute. I will not let her take this triumph from my hands. I notice my hands are now shaking violently and I grip my flute as hard as I can so the shaking will be less noticeable to the audience. The applause finally ends and I am free to leave the stage. In front of this vast audience, I feel lonelier than I ever have before. I think of saying goodbye to Allan. I think of the love this performance was to replace; the voice within me has kept me from that also. I sit in my dressing room with one small lamp on, which throws shadows of my face and silhouette of my flute against the wall. I stare at the black, flat figures on that wall and ask which is more real, they or I? Which has more life within its boundaries? Those shadows are what remain of my mind and my soul. I think about nothing for many minutes and then, looking away from the shadows, I determine to somehow find the help that I need. This concert was the kind of experience that makes one feel driven to choose between existence or nonexistence. I sit quietly and grimly, and say silently to myself, I choose existence.

Once I realize that I must seek professional help again, I talk over the serious problem with my family and resolve to search for that one psychiatrist that can help me. I knew I was much too trusting and I felt my illness was much too complex to find someone quickly, but I was determined to begin the search. I knew this search would be important and I realized that it could become a fight for which I needed the help of my parents. I decided that this would be a magnificent quest, one in which I would fight the great battles, just as Don Quixote, finding the objects of my search and destroying those that no longer belonged in society. In the best style of Don Quixote, I donned my armor and a sword I borrowed from a stagehand, and prepared myself to fight the windmills of my mind. I did not realize this quest would become so difficult. My mother and father took their positions at my side, as two well–equipped Sancho Panza's, to help me find the right windmills and the answers to my problem. Before my quest was through, I had been told the lies that one receives only from those who do not believe strongly enough in the nobility of the quest. I found, and I believed in my heart, I had destroyed eight monsters, in that holy search. I was diagnosed, or I should say misdiagnosed, with almost every malady known to man, from posttraumatic stress disorder to a local cold virus. Each psychiatrist offered a different reason for my problems and each wondered who had referred me to his specific "windmill". Each one had his or her own rigid set of medications, locked away in a secret box, as though they produced conjurer's spells and were to be protected at all costs. If these medications were but food I would have become the greatest gourmet of all time. At least, if they had been food I would have achieved the most pleasant of sensations to my palate rather than the large portion of disgust which left its taste in my mouth for months to come. Not only did the taste in my mouth appear to worsen, but my illness did also. I was told to be patient and that I needed to wait six to eight weeks for the medications to work. I would wait the standard six to eight weeks they always required desperate for relief; but the relief never came. Naturally I then asked the doctor for a change in medication, but instead of adjusting my medications I was simply made to feel like I was a genetic freak of nature.

NOTE: To all psychiatrists and other specialties, we are blessed with your presence and I appreciate the many sacrifices that you make in order to heal the sick. I have the highest respect for all of you except those few that I will write about shortly. I did, as you will see, finally find a doctor that had all of the skills necessary to treat me successfully, but for now I need to set all of you fine doctors aside and speak to those very few who have made it to the infamy of my own personal tome on the subject of psychiatric treatment.

Most artists know the great tome by Stanislavski which is titled *My Life In Art*. It actually changed the way we act today. I will probably not make such a strong impression on psychiatrists as Stanislavski's book did for actors, because unlike Stanislavski's book, this is a major treatise on how <u>not</u> to treat the mentally ill. So without any fanfare or further ado, I would like to give you a preview of my great work "My Life In Psychoanalysis".

My Life In Psychoanalysis
(A book within a book)

Introduction

There are many fine and talented psychiatrists well versed in their science, who were fine students in school and understand the vagaries of both Jung and Freud and the great disagreements between Gall and Wernicke. However, despite these noble and outstanding individuals, there are at least a few who should have probably left their diploma at the door upon leaving medical school.

   I believe that statistically, I probably have met more than my share of these fine but misguided gentlemen. Needless to say, with today's science, as we learn more and more about the brain, we find out that a good cigar really is just a good smoke, and that if psychoanalysis must rely on the patient's limited vocabulary to analyze the inner depths of his or her mind, it becomes something of a crap shoot to determine not only the source of the illness but the possible loci of damage within the complex organ we call the brain. The only thing worse than suffering with a severe brain disorder, is having to deal with physicians that have even greater problems than those of their patients. Having said all of this, let me give you a brief review of a few of the well meaning and studied professionals it has been my displeasure to meet during my quest for a cure.

Chapter 1: Dr. Coma

I drove three hours on one occasion to see a psychiatrist who I will call Dr. Coma, in the famed city of Beverly Hills. First of all there was no place to park. This was a beginning that reflected the rest of this adventure. Dr. Coma was supposed to be an "expert" at managing medications and I did not want to be late for our appointment, so instead of waiting the extra ten to twenty minutes it would have taken to find a parking space, I asked my parents to let me off at the curb. After circling the block for the fifth time, my parents slowed the car down enough to allow me to jump out onto the curb and look for his office. I rushed to the elevator and arrived at his second floor office EXACTLY ON TIME. His office had an outer sanctum and an inner sanctum separated by a wall with a small door and a button. I looked around for the receptionist but clearly the tiny waiting room did not contain one. There was a sign that said, "Please press button upon arrival". I expected the white rabbit to jump out at any moment, but in spite of that I pressed the button feeling much like Alice in Wonderland waiting for the rabbit to take me into his great fantasy world. Within a few minutes the door opened slightly. I fully expected a properly costumed receptionist but instead a rather sleepy looking doctor, his hair disheveled, poked his head into the room, looked around quickly as though for other patients and told me he would be "right with me". He then quickly shut the door. I then proceeded to wait over an hour. I expect that he was finishing croquet with the Queen. Just as I was getting ready to walk out, the doctor appeared again and looked around the tiny room once more for other patients. He apologized for the wait.

As I walked through the waiting room door, I was directed by the doctor to a room at the end of a short hallway. This at least was a larger room. It was filled with random piles of papers and clearly long forgotten notes. Sample bottles filled with medications not yet given to unsuspecting patients, lay strewn around the office in no particular order. I sat down and Dr. Coma asked me why I had come to see him. I looked slowly around the room and for the life of me I could not imagine why I had come. To my utter disbelief, as I was answering the question, his head fell to his chest and he fell fast asleep right in front of me. I did not know what to do. As he started to snore I asked in a loud voice that would hopefully stir him back to consciousness, "Is there a problem"? He woke up and acted like nothing had happened. Yes, I really was in Wonderland, I had come to the Mad Hatter's tea party and I was trying to have a conversation with the mouse who would come out of its sleep and rise up out of its cup just long enough to answer a question. He fell asleep numerous times during the course of our appointment; I stopped counting after fifteen. I asked repeatedly if I should come back later when he was feeling better. He kept insisting that he was fine, yet he kept falling asleep, sometimes while he himself was talking. After about 30 minutes of this, he woke up long enough to tell me "I don't know how you can stand being so sick, and "how did you manage to survive with such a terrible mental disorder"? Then he actually stated, "If I were you, I would have already killed myself".

When I got home I wrote him a scathing letter detailing everything that went on during our appointment and I reported him to the medical board. I got a letter back that I have kept to this day. Dr. Coma profusely apologized for his "drowsiness". He never once admitted that he had actually fallen asleep and the only excuse he offered for his extreme sleepiness was that he had been up all night with a sick patient.

Well, I have been up all night many times myself and nobody gets that tired after only going one night without sleep. I went on to see several more psychiatrists in what was starting to seem like a hopeless search for relief. At times I was so sick that I just accepted the doctors orders as gospel and would spend months under the care of a physician that had no idea how to treat my disorder.

Chapter 2: Dr. Perv

I soon met another one of these less than sterling examples of the modern healer. He was a doctor who struck me as a kind, caring individual with genuine empathy for his patients. I will call him "Dr. Perv". I was heartened by the fact that he did not seem to possess the stereotypical, cold, clinical, bedside manner. I felt fortunate that he seemed to truly listen to my problems. He made me feel less alone in the darkness of my disease, saying that we would find the solutions together, and in no time I would be skipping down the sunny trail to mental health. I saw this particular therapist once a week and for the first month of treatment I treaded water, getting neither better nor worse. Our therapy sessions seemed perfectly normal with the one troubling fact that each session was getting successively longer then the last. I was flattered by the fact that he seemed so interested in helping me. I had no idea that he was developing feelings for me that were entirely unprofessional.

As each appointment grew longer I started to get increasingly suspicious. Dr. Perv kept asking me more and more questions about my personal life and soon they got very personal, asking detailed questions about my love life and was I "currently dating anyone?" He also asked me what type of man I preferred to go out with. Dr. Perv's body language was also getting increasingly friendly. After a few weeks he began and ended our sessions with an amorous hug, which made me very uncomfortable, but in my very vulnerable and impressionable state, I attributed it to his seemingly caring nature. Things really started to degrade when during one session he tried to convince me that all my problems were caused by my family, which I did not believe. Dr. Perv tried to paint my family as the root of all evil, but I was unwilling to accept his diagnosis. I was confused by his attempt to diagnose what was clearly a mental illness as a social problem. Following this rather obscure social statement, leaving me with no direct analysis of my mental condition, he then followed this lack of professional psychiatric treatment by offering his medical office as a "temporary shelter" for me while I found a new place to live, in a more appropriate social environment. He even offered to give me a job "helping him around the office". Looking back on it, he was a very clever manipulator of women and before I knew it, he directly asked me for a date. I realized to my horror that he was not attempting psychiatric treatment so much as establishing his own personal dating service. He thought he had masterfully manipulated my emotions and kept me off balance enough to take advantage of my vulnerabilities. He looked genuinely surprised when I turned him down. Dr. Perv proved to be another psychiatrist who should seek employment in some other field of endeavor. Later, Dr. Perv was featured on a local news broadcast. He was being sued by several of his patients for sexual misconduct while under his care and even more horrifying, one of them was a minor. As you might have already guessed, Dr. Perv eventually lost his license to practice medicine.

Chapter 3: Dr. Kinder

Another interesting but fruitless therapy experience was with a well-meaning adult and child psychiatrist, accent on the "child", who I will call Dr. Kinder. He was a pleasant middle-aged man who unfortunately seemed unable to discern the age of his patients with any accuracy. All of his patients seemed to have a perceived age of 8 years. Each session he would speak to me as if I were a young child with questions like, "Can you tell me why your mommy doesn't like you to yell?" He always greeted me with a "How ya doin today sweetie" in a child like voice. Invariably, at the beginning of each appointment he would take a bowl of bonbons off his desk and wave it under my nose, asking me if I would like a piece of "yummy candy". Always looking disappointed when I refused his childish gifts of sugar, he would ask me if my "tum tum hurt?" My "tum tum" never hurt, but oh how my mind ached from the juvenile condescension that permeated our appointments. According to my physician, "Dr. Kinder", all of my problems were the result of "growing pains and separation anxiety". He could not have been more off base but he was right about one thing, I did have a serious case of "separation anxiety" as a result of my desperate need to be "separated" from his care as soon as humanly possible.

Chapter 4: Dr. Depressed

For all my dreadful experiences with twisted therapists the most disturbing was when I encountered a psychiatrist who was, even to the unschooled eye, in the throws of a very deep depression himself. For privacy's sake, I will call him Dr. Depressed. When I first met Dr. Depressed, he had a frighteningly sallow cast to his skin and his clothes looked as if he had slept in them all week. Over the next few weeks I watched as Dr. Depressed lived up to his name and soon the lines were blurred between doctor and patient. I would sit and listen to him complain to me about the terrible emotional pain in his life, sometimes for more than thirty minutes of our fifty–minute session. My only failing was that I did not have handy the proper pad and pencil with which to take notes. I felt terrible for Dr. Depressed, but the phrase "physician heal thyself" came to mind on more than a few occasions. It got to the point where I finally had to "terminate our relationship", as I was becoming increasingly worried that he was going to suicide on me! When I told him that I no longer felt comfortable having him treat me anymore because I felt I was doing all of the treating, he literally broke down in tears and I spent the entire appointment consoling him; scared out of my wits that I had pushed him right over the edge. I left Dr. Depressed's office for the last time after his tearful crisis half expecting to see his suicide on the 5:00 news and feeling guilty that I had abandoned him in his time of need. I left his care feeling completely drained and significantly more depressed.

Epilogue:

Comparatively speaking, a piece of "yummy candy" would have been a welcome offer at this point. However, I must admit I never sent him the professional bill expected for this type of treatment.

The Final Epilogue:

During the wasted years I spent with physicians that simply did not possess the skills to help me, my family was continually trying to get me to see what they called a "real specialist". I was often too sick, (a result of the many medical misdiagnoses), to recognize that better medical care was available and in the end just a few hours from my home.

The End

After my many failed attempts at locating a qualified professional who possessed the appropriate expertise to help me, I decided to remove my armor, place my borrowed sword in my closet and stop chasing windmills. Having tried numerous psychiatrists to no avail I began to search for physical causes. It had been three years now since I had lived with the first onslaught of the angry soprano. I went to my internist and asked for a complete physical and explained to him the type of problems I was having. My internist set out to remove any possible organic causes for the hallucinations I was experiencing. After many tests and diagnosis, the internist ruled out any possibility of organic causes such as a brain tumor. A brain tumor was something tangible, something I could blame for my symptoms, something I could have cut out, something that if it could not be cured would kill me and spare me a life filled with this kind of illness. I pictured myself locked up forever in some mental institution, talking to myself, lost to the world and living in my own very intricately woven reality that I could share with no one.

Over the next six months the angry soprano was becoming increasingly frequent, but more disturbing was the fact that her deafening non–sensical noises started to change to whole words. She was foul mouthed and words like "bitch" and "loser" and other words too profane to print were screamed at me over and over again. I would have to endure her yelling the same word over and over at me until I thought my head would explode.

I became extremely depressed once the soprano started saying words I could recognize. Up until she started yelling words at me that I could understand clearly, I had myself convinced that I could live with the unintelligible noises. I tried to calm my emotions regarding this voice that would not leave my mind. Having not been able to find an answer I could live with, my brain set about to rationalize into existence a set of excuses for why I had a voice within my head. I came up with many different rationalizations. I rationalized that lots of people have to live with tinitus, (a disorder that leaves a person with high pitched ringing in their ears that never goes away), and I reasoned, if they could lead productive lives then I could certainly live with the angry soprano and lead a productive life also. Time and again I tried to be dispassionate about the voice I was hearing and tried to analyze it in some way that would relieve the frustration and anxiety of the situation. After the angry soprano's words began, I decided to keep a journal in the hopes of discovering just what was causing the voice. I was convinced, in my sick mind, that if I could just find some pattern or some precipitating factor that was always present right before she started one of her "concerts", I could somehow bend the voice to my Will and silence her forever. This was the ultimate rationalization.

I kept the journal as faithfully as I could for well over a year. Each time the voice started I would write down what I had been doing prior to the event. The desperation to find that certain something that would trigger the screaming permeated my journal entries. I found myself obsessively writing down every little detail of what I had been doing and thinking just prior to the event, afraid to leave out even the smallest detail for fear that I would miss that one piece of information that would hold the key to silencing the mocking voice in my head. My journal entries from that time were filled with what I now recognize as meaningless trivialities, but at the time each tiny scrap of information held deep meaning for my desperate mind. The following is an entry from that journal:

> *I always put my thoughts in parenthesis so I could go back later and easily distinguish between an action and a thought for later analysis.*
>
> *Monday 9:40 am—The word today is <u>"bitch"</u> (I wish she would find a new word!) The voice started in with "bitch, bitch, bitch" while I was in the woman's bathroom in the mall. Before she started I looked in the mirror to check my hair. (Don't like my hair today). I am wearing a black pantsuit with black earrings today. I don't like the fabric (it is scratchy). She screams " bitch, bitch, bitch" ever louder. I looked down at the sink to wash my hands. The soap container over the first sink was empty (frustrating). So I walked to the second sink and used the soap dispenser over that sink. The sinks are white and they are surrounded by black tile. (I like the tile but it bothers me that it shows even the tiniest bit of dirt). I pressed the soap squirter 2 times, the soap was pink and very thick and a bit gritty. The soap was in my right hand first. The soap did not foam very easily, (frustrating). I rubbed my hands together, I think 11 times and then I rinsed my hands off in the second sink. I could not get all of the soap off so I used the warm water after turning the cold water off. (The faucets were*

dirty). The water continued to run for a few seconds after I walked away from the sink. (I worried it was stuck but it turned off). I got a paper towel to dry my hands. I used three paper towels (they were also scratchy) and I put them in the trashcan next to the door. The trashcan was full, (I worried the paper towels would not stay in the trashcan because it was filled to the top, but they did). I grabbed the door handle, which felt cold to me, and at that point the voice screamed even louder, "bitch, bitch, bitch, bitch, bitch, bitch!" Perhaps I am too tired today, I did not get very much sleep last night, that makes nine days in a row. END OF JOURNAL ENTRY (I never could find that one thread that connected all of those so–called "concerts" together. I remember asking myself– What kind of being was it that is buying me a front row seat to its many tirades?)

The angry soprano begins screaming obscenities at me day and night. It is maddening trying to keep track of all of the "evidence" I am trying to analyze. I review my journal over and over, studying each word and phrase trying to find new insights into the reasons for the angry soprano's intrusions into my life. I could be so happy if only she would disappear. I might go for a month feeling normal and just as I begin to feel safe she would appear again. After a while it became too exhausting trying to write down every tiny detail of the minutes and sometimes hours before the appearance of the angry voice.

I try a variety of things to make the angry soprano end her concert early or keep her off the stage of my mind, but nothing seems to work. Next, I try drowning her out with my Walkman radio. I turn up the volume as far as I can and still stand it, but even then I can hear her screaming over the sounds of the radio, "bitch…, whore…, bastard, there's a sewer, step into it!, see if you can stick you head in the water, do it now you bastard!" The voice would not be denied her audience. Damn her voice, damn her presence, damn her reality. This is my head, this is my mind, this is my life. This angry voice needs to understand that it must get out of my reality. I can't think of enough words about her raucousness, her crudeness, and her lack of sensitivity to express well her influence on my entire existence. The words fail me. Hate is a very weak word for the emotion I feel at this moment and I cannot even reach for her throat to begin to choke the life out of her vicious being. Her words are like a giant knife that cleaves through the center of my soul and leaves a gaping void that I cannot fill through any thoughts or actions. I inevitably became very depressed again and angry with everyone and everything around me. I take my anger out on those I can touch and feel outside of my being.

I worry constantly that I will be "found out" and my performance career will be over. After living with the horrors of the Tarantella, the visions of my dead grandfather and my dead grandmother, the presence of the angry soprano helped open the floodgates of my mind for every horrid hallucination my fatigued brain could conjure up. I was to suffer from delusions with a cast of hundreds, filling my alternate reality with nightmarish scenes of a disorganized world filled with cruelty, torture, gruesome images and the chaotic colorations of a stupefying nightmare. These delusions left the peaceful continuity and constancy of the real world far behind. Images could appear from nowhere and intermingle with a staccato of sound and vibrancy, which did not depend in any way on the smooth undulations of reality's characteristic images, sounds and inherent continuity. Just imagine for a second, a reality, which has gaping black holes scattered around a sunlit pastoral scene, where the sun could start to set and a flashing moon in narrow crescent would take its place, or imagine a place where bushes that were green turned red as they moved in response to breezes which turned to hurricanes, which turned to gentle breezes once again in the blink of a bloodshot, half–opened eye. Imagine having a delightful conversation about the summer weather with a friend, who stands grinning and agreeing with you and then disappears in mid–sentence, leaving only a wall of old bricks where large Black Widows emerge and fill the shadow left by your friend. This was my alternate reality and it became stronger with each passing day. It became more persistent in crowding out the normalcy of my true reality. This made any kind of living unbearable. It also had a great impact on my concert work. Conductors that I worked with on a regular basis, were at a loss as to why my performances were not up to their usual high standards, and my flute students wondered why I was progressively apathetic during their lessons.

As the delusions worsened, my memory became severely impaired and my ability to concentrate on any one thing for more than a few seconds was impossible. I would lose music two minutes after setting it down somewhere. I forgot rehearsal times and to my utter disbelief I would actually forget to practice my flute. My depression became so severe that it was almost impossible to get any practicing done at all. I would sit for hours in front of a score on my music stand, just staring into space, often daydreaming about the sweet relief that suicide could provide for me.

In the midst of my deepest psychosis, I receive a call from Maestro Sanduval, who again asks me to play a solo performance. This time he asks me to play the vast, expansive and beautiful 20th century work, for Flute and Orchestra by Nielsen. I know the music well and I know that it will demand the best that I have within me to be able to communicate its intricate and complex musical statements. I quickly say, "yes" to the maestro, knowing that I will have to fight myself, as well as the music, in order to reach out beyond my own inner torment and communicate the composer's statement of life's emotions. The stage was set for the battle of my life.

4

A Mind's Crazy Cadenza

Messages from An Alternate Reality

Since my loss of Allen's love, I still feel I must fill my soul with the music of my performances. I am resolved to make my next performance of Nielsen's Concerto the best I have ever done. I begin preparations for this new concert with a fervor and an energy that I have never applied before, determined to fill my soul with the sounds of my music so that I may replace the emptiness left by the love I have lost. Now begins the exercises, and readings of the music and at the same time, the endless preparations needed to produce a flawless performance. All this was the normal prelude to a concert. But this special time I would add one more great preparation that will call on all of my body, my mind and my soul itself. This will be my life's greatest battle to regain my will, my mind, and my reason for being. I am prepared to meet the demons head on and emerge triumphant or die in the trying.

I began the new schedule of rehearsals, resolute in my determination to carry out the practice session in defiance of the angry soprano. At the rehearsals, I vacillate between being ridiculously manic or horribly depressed, sometimes several times in one day. I try to respond quickly and without question to the many increasing demands of the conductor without showing these alternating states. I determine that at home, I must organize my home life as perfectly as I will prepare for the Nielsen. In order to do that, I begin to prepare long, organized lists of things to do to help me perform at home as well as in concert. Little do

I realize, that my illness has driven me once more to mania. My organization at home becomes obsessive. I have always kept home as a safe haven from the difficulties of public rehearsals and performances but now in my desire to reach perfection both in the concert hall and at home, I begin a series of manic exercises to organize my home life more perfectly than ever.

My mania was driving me to merge both my concert world and my home world, into one glorious and perfect organization of actions and musical performance. I would leave unending Post It Notes everywhere reminding me of all of the tasks I had to accomplish that day, and I would set the meeting alarm on my computer to remind me of rehearsals and lessons scheduled. I left notes inside drawers, on the outside of drawers, in my appointment book, on my computer monitor, on my adding machine, on sheets of paper, on my desk trays, on my music stand, on my flute case, in my purse, in my wallet, on my file cabinet, on my phone: anywhere I could see a message, I left one hoping that if I had enough reminders in my line of sight, I would be able to complete all of the tasks for that day efficiently and accurately. However, this manic list took me beyond what any human can attain, giving me tasks that took far more than the twenty four hours that anyone has in a single day. I felt sure that I would be able to complete all of the tasks for that day, efficiently and accurately, and still have time to rehearse, not only the Nielsen, but untold numbers of scores. Some days it did not matter how many little reminders I left around, I would not see them because I had forgotten their existence. I left so many notes I gave up reading many of them. Instead, I would think about the music; contemplating variations on its themes, forgotten as quickly as I composed them and never really concentrating on the music itself.

While practicing for the upcoming concerto I would stay in a manic state for days at a time making it doubly hard to prepare for this important concert. I gave up all sense of musical reality as I lived for these brief periods of jubilant emotions that come with such manic states. For me, mania was my reward, a gift given to me by my tortured mind to allow me to endure the atrocious periods of depression and hallucinations. The feelings of jubilation I experienced while I was in a manic state were exaggerated beyond normal reality and can only be described as abnormal.

During these manic periods my mind was constantly subjected to this type of euphoria and I welcomed it like the beauty of Mozart's 40th Symphony. When manic, I felt such a sense of intense joy, that I viewed the world in an entirely different way; anything I wanted to achieve was suddenly within my reach. My mania was accompanied by an endless energy that coursed through my body as if my adrenal glands were set to run round the clock, accelerating my body and mind to a ridiculously fast tempo.

Mania, as I have said before, is the torturer's short respite to make the rest of the torture even more unbearable, but of course I could not see that dire ending to this state. My mania drew me to my flute, just as an actor who loses the boundary between make believe and reality brings home his costume to continue to play out the written scenes within his home, so too I would continue to play my flute as though still on the stage, without any audience except those who existed in my own personal reality. I would spend days reading through piece after piece in my music library, and as I played, each note felt as if it was being performed to perfection. My mania masked the truth from me, substituting mediocrity for the performance level I was capable of in a normal state and blinding me to the slow descent of my mind, into the troughs of this unreal amusement park. My mania made every phrase seem perfect to me; every interpretation appeared to be brilliant. Somehow my tone seemed purer and stronger than I ever imagined. This was the extent to which my unreality masked the truth of my degrading performances. I truly felt that I was producing inspired music making and I could find not a single flaw in my playing. In my manic world, I believed that I could play better than anyone else in the universe. My mind presented a false concert to my ears, tricking me into believing that I had superior control over my dynamics and breath support. While in this manic state, I would make recording after recording of my practice sessions, believing that such perfection should not be wasted; I believed I owed it to the world to record for posterity, my brilliant tone and technique for all the world to enjoy for all eternity. My mania had succeeded with its masquerade. My eyes and my ears, saw and heard only those images and sounds that my mental disorder allowed.

While manic, I often drove my family into frantic states of exasperation. Members of my family would tell me over and over again to slow down, my mother would warn me about the dangers of my mood swings. She would yell at me for playing my flute at 4am, but I didn't hear her, even when she stood right in front of me, lips moving, voice raised to a strained tenor. She made absolutely no impression on me while I played along with Mahler #4 blasting in the background; I could hear nothing but bar after bar of fortissimo phrases, filled with a forceful melding of percussion, winds, strings and brass. I was no longer aware of human conversation.

In this state of heightened mania, I always had a pressing need to get "things" done. I would make impossible lists, unintelligible graphs and charts outlining all of the vitally important things that I needed to get done in the foreseeable future in an obsessive attempt to over–plan the limited hours I had at home. I had so many brilliant ideas and so much to offer the world when manic, I could hardly get it all down on paper fast enough.

I have included here, a typical list I made each day during this manic state. I constantly made changes to the daily list I generated since my priorities seemed to shift, sometimes almost minute to minute, forcing me to rethink the list again and again; erasing, rewriting, condensing and/or elaborating until the words on the paper were hardly legible. The "Forty or Bust" in the following list refers to a contest I would have with myself each day. I believed that if I didn't get forty things done each day, then I had effectively wasted twenty–four hours I could never reclaim. I invariably did get forty things done but they were rarely on the list and they rarely contributed to my health, my music or my organization. Ironically, I often would forget the list as soon as I put it down and would just float from one fragmented fugue state to the next, until by chance I would remember the list, at which time I'd resume the tasks I'd so meticulously written down, at least until my mind started another list.

Things to do today!! Forty or Bust

1. Record all Faure and the Frank sonata—Use the International editions

2. Record the 25 excerpts for students–think about a cover for the tape

3. Record the Paganini studies for students

4. Record the Prokofiev Sonata

5. Call accompanist—see if she can work an extra 2 hours today

6. Practice at least 8 hours today!

7. Write down new tone exercises for flute book

8. Clean house

9. Clean car

10. Clean flute, get new polishing cloth

11. Call about concert on 18th

12. Finish drawings of new flute cleaning device

13. Finish drawings of new flute sack

14. Go look at fabrics for Flute Sack

15. Organize my music library

16. Do my laundry

17. Iron my concert dress

18. Clean my piccolo

19. Organize files on computer

20. Brush the cat

21. Clean out shower

22. Start writing tonal exercise book

23. Pick some flowers for mom

24. Sharpen all the pencils in my flute bag

25. Learn the Cello

26. Learn the Recorder

27. Clean out closet

28. Prepare the scores for rehearsal

29. Organize jewelry

30. Buy supplies for flute stand invention

31. Research the patent potential of invention

32. Program a new recital

33. Call for concert hall availability

34. Prepare press releases for new recital

35. Listen to new flute recordings for competition

36. Organize desk

37. Call conductor to discuss concerto

38. Call for flute maintenance in Boston

39. Feed my fish

40. Clean out my fish tank

Reading this list, any rational observer can easily see that the tasks listed required many more than twenty-four hours to complete, and certainly could not be accomplished by someone who is suffering from severe sleep depravation and psychosis. But to the new improved, manic, perfect and super human me, the "Forty or Bust" list was a reasonable plan to make sure I was organized enough to complete the pressing needs at home and in rehearsal. When manic, I became extremely concerned about musicians' rights. I developed an obsessive feeling of empathy towards all musicians which was indescribably sensitive and deep, and although it reflects my love of music, it was nonsense created by my mania. This obsessive feeling of empathy towards all musicians is indescribable, but it all made so much sense to me when I was manic.

As the mania subsided, my mind returned to a more consonant state but I was left feeling empty and drained. It was as though my mind had a damper on it, reducing the vibrations in my brain, much like a damper on the strings of a piano. My brain was no longer energized and alive, it felt dead, motionless and clouded as depression set in to cover my mind once again with its insidious mantle.

Under the influence of this returning depression, I would review the "amazing recordings" I had made while manic and listen in horror to the atrociousness of the playing recorded. The supple tone I thought I had and the flawless technique I believed I possessed, were nowhere to be heard on these recordings. I sounded just like one might expect a tired, exhausted flutist to sound who had gone without sleep for three days straight and had played her flute for sixteen hours at a time. In these pitiful recordings, it was clear that my lip muscles and therefore embouchure were gone. You could hear me taking huge gasping breaths, as I chopped phrases into unintelligible pieces. In some cases, I did not even recognize the piece I had recorded because it was so distorted. My playing, colored by the twisted mask of manic grandiosity, had deafened my ears to the horrendously terrible performances I had recorded. Later, I would destroy the recordings in a flood of tears realizing what I had done.

As my depression worsened, practicing became an exercise in slow motion, and I felt as if I were playing in a large room filled with sticky, soft marshmallows. My fingers moved, but only very slowly over the keys. At times, I would stop the Nielsen and begin playing any of the ten to twenty scores I kept on my music stand for ready access during this period. My mind conjured reasons to perfect each of these pieces.

Some days, I would look at my flute case and imagine the beauty, the sheer exquisite, ultimate beauty of my flute in its case, but I could not bring myself to touch that beloved instrument. I would repeatedly hold the case against my head, straining to hear the notes of the concerto I was soon to play, but instead hearing only the sounds of my breathing and the mindless words from the voice inside my head. Sometimes I would walk past my music stand and take one of the parts with me to my bedroom and lie with the music over my face on my bed, trying to absorb the blur of notes on the page by some sort of new osmotic process. I would try to will the notes from the page into my mind where I could memorize the delicate sounds of Nielsen. I would quietly sing the melody, making silent notes to myself about an accidental here, and a breath mark there. I often would sob as I attempted to practice the melodic line in my head. It was a resigned sob, the kind when one finally accepts ones future fate and has but to wait for its terrible, inevitable conclusion. I would try to concentrate on five to ten bars in this state and then would quietly settle on a single note. This note would resonate inside my head, suspended as if a fermata sign were written above it. I would lose track of time and my mind would cycle as though an endless loop tape was playing the same note over and over again, while my consciousness was saturated with that angry soprano's voice telling me I was a "terrible musician—a terrible person." The daily internal machinations were causing bloodless hemorrhages in my mind and I was destitute of human feelings.

Despite the difficulty, I was driven to continue working. I had to rehearse. I had to make this my best performance yet. I rejected help when it was offered. I had to win this war. I knew that in completing this performance I would be able to get rid of this angry voice within my mind.

It is my love for the Nielsen Concerto and the fact that I have played the piece so many times before, that leads me to the false assumption that even though I am exhausted from the depression and the hallucinations, Nielsen's beautiful music will carry tonight's rehearsal performance for me. I make a half-hearted attempt before the 7:00pm rehearsal to warm up, running through some scales and arpeggios. Trying to warm up through the deep fog of depression is exhausting and after ten minutes I am spent. I think about doing some long tone exercises, but it is all I can do to clean out my flute and put it back in its case. I have to save my energy for rehearsal. I will need every ounce of strength to fight the ugly voice that will surely be raging within my mind tonight.

All afternoon I have been hopeful because the angry soprano has not made an appearance since early morning. I believe that God has finally taken pity on me and intervened on my behalf, allowing me to have some desperately needed clarity of thought in rehearsal.

As I drive the hour and a half to the concert hall, I have plenty of time to think about all of the things that could go wrong. The familiar feelings of anxiety that seem to color all of my performance experiences lately come flooding into my mind as I pull into the parking lot. This is to be one of only two rehearsals I will get with the orchestra and I cannot afford to waste it. As I walk into the concert hall I can hear the orchestra warming up.

I step over to the conductor and speak briefly with him about questions I have regarding tempi and needed cues; I feel exhausted just from the ride and I have not even begun to rehearse. My whole body is shaking as I take my flute case out of my bag and look briefly around the hall to see if anyone notices the desperate level of my agitation.

My senses, which have been rubbed raw by my mental state, are aware of even the slightest movement and sound. Even the slightest whisper of unwanted sounds in my head increases the trembling of my body and now my hands, as I connect the three sections of my flute together. I silently try to reassure myself. I try every type of old performance trick I have learned to settle my pre–performance nerves. Some of my special tricks work temporarily to calm the shaking. In spite of my condition, I manage to get my flute together and place it on the chair next to me as I begin to search for my sheet music for the Nielsen. I must use this music because I can no longer memorize the notes of the concerto. My illness has forced me to give up playing from memory.

When I first started having problems with my memory, I rejected the notion of using music; to me it was a sign of weakness. For some time I relied on my brain's motor memory, allowing it to control the motion of my fingers. If I drew a blank during the performance of a piece, I relied on my motor memory and my subconscious to keep my fingers playing the correct notes. After countless hours of practicing, I could play a piece without any conscious awareness of moving my fingers. Unfortunately, as I became increasingly ill, even my tired brain could not make up for the ever–increasing lapses of memory and my fingers lost their direction. Pieces that I had played from memory many times in the past, had begun to elude me as my ability to concentrate for extended periods of time gradually eroded.

The act of memorizing music through the muddy thick fog in my mind, became an arduous task, and soon even trying to memorize a single page of music became an insurmountable chore. I was angry with myself, mostly because this was another battle I had lost with the angry soprano and the illness which was slowly paralyzing me. But I still wanted to perform. So, grudgingly, I began to use music in all of my concerto work. I do not want my image or my arms, or my body, or my mind, to continue to be crippled in this way. I will fight the loneliness that it gives me. I will fight the love it has taken from me. I will fight for the dignity it has destroyed. I will stay a free human being. I will fight the pain and I will not give up the human qualities that I treasure. I will get through this performance. I will defeat the voice. I will. I will.

I find the score and holding my head high and my flute in a confident position for all to see, I walk to the music stand and place the score just so, readying myself for the performance. I stand behind the music stand, raise my flute to my mouth and play a few tentative notes to better understand the special acoustics of the hall. I listen for the reverberations and the quality of the echoing sounds they bring back to my ears. The shaking in my hands diminishes slightly, as I begin to focus my attention on the music rather than on the uncontrolled madness. I play through a few bars of the final movement to reassure myself that I can move through this rehearsal successfully and without revealing my inner turmoil to the other players. The conductor waits patiently at the podium as I make my final preparations. With one final glance towards me and then the orchestra, he lifts his baton to signal the orchestra to begin. I listen as the orchestra plays the rapid and stirring introduction by Nielsen. I notice that as the Nielsen begins there is no sign of activity from the voice within my head. I stand facing the orchestra, which I prefer to do in rehearsal. This orientation helps me to maintain the ensemble playing required for this piece. My body tenses now as my entrance nears. I lift my flute to my lips and begin to play the forceful, marcato descending line which creates the powerful opening statement for the concerto. My mind and my heart and my fingers focus on every note bringing technique and articulation to center stage and sending the notes singing over the head of the conductor to the very back of this great hall. I try to lose myself in the act of communicating the great emotions evoked by the music. I begin to lose all sense of myself and become totally involved in this concerto that means so much to me in my battle to save my soul.

As the music continues, I feel the emotions of the music playing through my body. My heart and my soul are already filled with this moving music and I am lost in those special emotions that only great music can create for the musician in performance. Musicians are the instruments through which pure emotions are communicated, and therefore I stand naked and vulnerable when I perform. My emotions become raw and exposed, and the notes like fingers gently touching my body, to produce an effect like no other. It is as though I am on stage in the midst of my most intimate actions, unable to either hide my emotions or the effect they appear to project on the audience. I am as vulnerable as I would be with my lover during this type of performance. It is because of this type of exposure that I am also most vulnerable to the demons in my mind. In spite of knowing this, I continue to perform my music with everything I have within my body and my mind and throwing to the winds of chance, the possibility that my illness will choose this moment to begin its attack.

By the end of the first movement, with all of my defenses down, I begin to hear an almost imperceptible sound in my head; a pitch, slightly off key, which gains strength little by little. I continue to play with all the strength I have available to me, but I realize that I am fighting myself and the creatures created by my own sick reality. The voice is clear now. It is the angry soprano, speaking to me as though from a far distance, calling out vulgarisms, calling out loser. My mind becomes saturated with these sounds. I fight to hear the orchestra over the vulgar language and for an instant I see a large, long black spider leg performing those sharp stuttering movements, so familiar to me, as it tries to find its pray from behind the timpani. I try with everything left within me to fight this increasing battle and I attempt to concentrate on the music in front of me as the voice in my head abruptly shifts from a whisper to a brutal scream. I continue to stand firmly in front of my music, not knowing how to respond but desperately trying to maintain a good ensemble with the orchestra. Then, the screaming soprano increases the intensity of her cruel insults, yelling over and over again "You are a loser, you are a loser, YOU <u>ARE</u> A LOSER!" I try even harder not to let on that there is a problem, but I have been left exposed too long by the sound of the music. The soprano, sensing my weakened condition, continues her attack upon my helpless mind. But I have no choice, as excruciating as the torture has become, I feel I must complete the piece; my sanity, perhaps my very life depends on it.

In this silent battle, between myself and this evil creature, I begin to hear the angry soprano hum just slightly off key with the orchestra. She knows full well that my cadenza is coming. She knows full well that I am standing before the orchestra, tied to the upright post of my destruction, forced to play a cadenza which she will not let me freely play. The conductor motions to me with his baton for the beginning of my cadenza. Before I have hit the first note, I recall the many words I have had with this conductor about the interpretation of this cadenza and the feelings it must portray. This conductor is driven by the same need to communicate his music as I, and is even willing to physically draw from my very soul, the true essence of the notes.

As I begin to play the cadenza, the voice inside me yells strong epithets at the conductor. Even though only I can hear them, I wince with the pain of their sharp inanities and vulgarisms, "That stupid jerk does not know how to conduct, he needs to break that damned baton over his head, play the damn cadenza now, play it as loud as you ever have, blow away the stupid bastard, he shouldn't be conducting this piece, he doesn't know the music, play the cadenza, play. Play. PLAY!" As though in response to these outcries, I take a deep breath and begin playing the notes of the cadenza, but it is no longer my fingers that are playing. It is the angry soprano in her full glory, forcing me to drive through the debris of the notes left by the composer; to shove my way past them into a new nightmarish freedom. My fingers fly ever more rapidly over the keys with the unwanted aid of this angry voice inside of me, controlling my every movement. I begin to play an increasingly violent rendition of the original music; somehow I am creating a nether world of sounds not given to me by Nielsen's music. The sounds move farther and farther away from the consonance that one would expect from an instrument in the normal, unbroken continuity of reality.

I am no longer aware of my fingers movements as the music flies from my flute, past the conductor and slams into the back walls of the empty hall. I can hear the unearthly reverberation of the sounds, as though it is an organ playing its own remembrance of Bach in a key yet to be determined. I can vaguely hear the conductor snapping his baton on the music stand, rapidly at first and then violently, until he adds his voice in unison with each beat of the baton snapping over and over again, stop, stop, stop. I finally become aware of his angry command and the life leaves my fingers. The flute drops to my side, as I clutch one end loosely in my hand. I stare at the conductor, almost vacuously, not really seeing him and not understanding fully what I have just played. The conductor, staring angrily up at the ceiling, shakes his head in disgust and walks off stage, and I am left there standing dumb before the orchestra. The conductor's assistant interrupts the silence as he yells for a ten–minute break. I turn around quickly without looking at any of the members of the orchestra and leave the hall, not to return.

I run to the parking lot and quickly jump into my car and throw my flute into the back seat. I want to be gone from this place as soon as possible, I can think of nothing else. I start the engine and race frantically towards the safety of my home. Maybe, if I drive fast enough, I can leave the voice behind. Maybe if I drive fast enough, I can throw the spiders to the wind. Maybe if I can drive fast enough, I can outrun this madness. All of the emotions that I had tried to keep under control, burst forth spilling over my body and out onto the road. It is very cold outside but I roll down my window anyway. I need fresh air to drive away the putrid smell of my dark thoughts and misused feelings. The wind is sharp and biting as it gusts across my face. The endless flow of tears streaming down my cheeks are led on arbitrary paths across my features until the salty beads of water merge and are finally ripped away from my flesh without mercy. My thoughts are in disarray, reflections of happier days merge with confusing images of large ungodly beasts and sinister disorienting sounds swirling chaotically around in my mind. I crane my head out the window as far as my neck will allow, my muscles cramping from tendons stretched to their snapping point. I <u>must</u> reside in the cold wind and the tears; they connect me with the reality that my demons try to push aside. Reality is not the dark, deafening voice in my brain that is commanding me to leap from my speeding car onto this hectic freeway. It is this unreality that I must fight. I must continue to feel the wetness on my cheeks and the stinging wind that pushes against my face to save what is left of my reality. The stinging wind is real. My tears strengthen my reality.

As I speed down the freeway, far in excess of the posted limits, I try desperately to distinguish between the blissful serenity of truth and the terrifying furor of delusion. The musty strained voice in my head continues its endless commands like a cursed loop tape. Over and over, I am told to open the door and jump out of my car. It does not matter to the dark voice in my delusion that I will die if I do as I am told and yet I am inexplicably compelled to follow its pitiless commands. I put my hand on the handle of my car's door. I open the door slightly; I peer down at the asphalt rushing past me. I start to open the door the rest of the way. If I let go of the wheel and leap out of this car made of tons of steel and glass, how many lives will perish with mine? Will my family find me broken and misshapen on the asphalt and cause the hollow tendrils of grief to wind round their souls and destroy them also? How many lives will perish with mine? I press my foot on the accelerator as I slam the door shut.

I will not follow these commands. I will not become the helpless slave of this voice within my mind. I <u>must</u> think of something else. I must stay in touch with reality. I must focus on the coolness of the air stream on my face and neck. I remind myself that this is what reality feels like, uncomfortable at times, cold and filled with ambivalence at times, but reality nonetheless. I would much rather exist in the genuine world than relinquish my inner thoughts to a disorienting madness that warps my mind and strips me of the essence of who I am and what I am. This voice, this madness may drive me into the cloak of death. If that happens, will my nonexistence replace this horror with something more gentle and less terrifying? Oh, how I will miss my family when I am gone; their sweet calming touches and gentle reassurances that tomorrow will be better than today. Reality dictates that I must pull over. Reality dictates that I must stop this car before psychosis becomes reality. I turn on the air conditioner to add to the already cold air swirling around me and I remind myself that cold air equals reality, cold air equals sanity. Through the twisted circuitry in my brain and the cacophony of distorted sounds, I speak out loud to myself, "cold air, slower speed, cold air, slower speed, cold air, pull over, cold air, pull over, cold air, stop, cold air, stop. Sitting by the side of the road, I cling to even the tiniest details of reality, the rustle of my polyester windbreaker, the sound of my own labored breathing. I am still here. I am still O.K. I still possess reason. I must have some chards of my ruptured sanity left. I am still in the here and now. I turn off the ignition and start to cry. The car is now motionless and I will not find death by jumping out of it. My madness has not consumed me today. As I sit in the car waiting for my body to stop uncontrollably shaking, the tears begin gathering at the base of my chin and gravity beckons them to separate from the sadness of my face. I hear the tears land on the sleeve of my jacket in an agreeable staccato, much as rain on an open umbrella, creating whimsical star–like patterns on the fabric. It is my heart crying for the warm soothing arms of reality.

It takes hours to pull myself together as I sit shaking in my car by the side of the road. I am numb to the outside world until a large truck passes me at a high rate of speed making a booming sound as it passes frighteningly close to me, shaking my vehicle from the wind compression between our two vehicles. As if waking from a nightmare, I quickly start the car and drive home. I arrive at home shaking from exhaustion, I feel utterly spent and fall into bed, knowing that I must sleep. But once again I am awakened in the darkness by another dreaded hallucination. I sit up stiffly in bed and realize that the Tarantella has begun once again. Drained of any remaining life and without the strength to do battle a deep hopelessness sets in, and I resolve then and there to die. There, in that darkened room after my failure at the rehearsal and my battle lost to that voice, I slowly proceed to try and hang myself in my closet with one of my belts. I briefly stop to put on a record of my favorite flute sonata by Cesar Frank. I listen quietly to the first sounds of the piano, a prelude to the flute entrance. I then calmly attach one end of the belt to the clothing rod in my closet and with the other end of the belt I make a noose. The rod is not high enough for me to freely hang, but I am resolved to choke myself to death no matter what, even if it means slowly smothering to death while my shins touch the floor, at least I will receive the final peace that I so long for at this moment. Sobbing, I let my legs go limp. I can feel the noose tighten around my windpipe and I can sense my pulse pounding in my temples. My lips feel like they are expanding, and the pressure I feel in my head is building. Suddenly, without warning, the closet rod breaks free from the wall and sobbing I fall to the floor along with all of the clothing hanging from the rod, in a single jumble of emotions and cloth. I sit there numbly with the belt still tightly wrapped around my neck continuing to cry, not believing that even in this macabre performance I have failed myself once again. I sit on the floor of my closet, dazed and defeated. The belt still hangs from my neck. I begin to sob a slow, deep, lonely sob, which cries out wordlessly of the utter desolation of my life and the abandonment of my soul. With all the strength left in my body, I slowly stand up and remove myself from the closet. I realize now, that even my death will require the preparation needed for all great performances. So, there on my bed in the middle of the night I set about planning for my death. Determined that it will be as perfect as the Nielsen Concerto could have been.

In the evenings following my attempted suicide, I rehearse Nielsen with all the frantic vigor of someone caught near the end of his or her exit from life. I can picture the hall of my death even as I plan for it. Center stage is the conductor, full of life; trying to draw from my tired instrument the fullness of the composer's creation and at stage left is death beckoning me from the darkness of the wings to complete my concert under his direction. During the day I carefully plan for my departure from this earth. I wanted it to be my last great performance, thinking in my distorted mind that somehow people would appreciate finding me in calm repose as though in the midst of a static performance, frozen in time, prepared for the playing of the music in my finest clothing.

I carefully choose my best blue suit and matching blue shoes. I starch the suit and iron it more carefully than any suit I had ever ironed before. Then I lay it out, just so, on my couch, where I can look at its perfection and savor the performance in which I will be found lying lifeless in these beautiful blue clothes. I find matching blue earrings with a fine fluted silver edging which I polish carefully, so that if my head is turned to the side in death, the light will glint from their decorated edges to bring attention to how beautiful I look in the arms of death. I decide to wear white underwear, so that when they finally undress me, they will discover the virginity which my body still holds within it. I finish this magnificent costume with a blue scarf and matching purse so that people will understand that my life has been a wonderful performance and not the failed waste that it was. I make plans for my Last Will and Testament and place the words upon a cream colored paper, not white because unlike my body these words are no longer virgin. I carefully fold the Last Will and Testament in thirds to signal its spiritual importance as represented within the numerology of distant times. Three represents the Holy Trinity and it also represents my lost love, my flute and the music that I will never play again. I make up a short list of those last things needed for my final performance. The list read as follows:

Death Day

Clothing to wear:

- *Blue Suit (iron it with starch) and pair with blue heels*
- *White underwear*
- *Blue earrings with silver edging (polish)*
- *Blue wallet and purse*

Last Will and Testament:

- *Print out on cream colored paper and make envelope*
- *Place in envelope that is addressed to "My Loving Family"*
- *Place envelope in Purse, put in outside pocket*

Knife:

- *Buy Exacto blades and get blade handle from our office*
- *Bring 2 extra blades in case they break easily*
- *Bring picture of neck anatomy for jugular vein location*

Time:

- *Get cab and go at 8:00 am to Montecito cemetery,*

Place:

- *Montecito Cemetery, highest lot location*

- *Go to large mausoleum on top of hill overlooking ocean*
- *Sit down behind mausoleum against wall facing ocean, place purse with Will on lap*

Tape Recorder:

- *Bring tape recorder and headphones with recording of Chopin Concerto, second movement.*
- *Complete the performance.*

I slowly sign my name at the bottom of this morbid list, Tracy Lynn Harris, Concert Flutist and below that I add, "Please God forgive me all of my sins and grant me successful passage to Heaven".

I expected my audience to consist of my family and then later perhaps doctors and law enforcement officers of various types. Surely my family would see that death was truly the only alternative for me. I carefully write the following letter to be left placed just so in my purse for my family to read:

> *I can't take this anymore. I am useless at work and I am useless to my family. I need to die, it is not a matter of should I die, I need to die. I can't feel like this even one more day. I know that you will come to understand in time. I just don't understand how I allowed my life to get so out of control. At least that noisy voice in my head will go with me, a modicum of revenge on this illness! I kept asking God to answer my prayers and kill me on the way to work. A car accident would have been just the thing and at least you would not have to live with the fact that I killed myself: my final insult. I have brought you so much pain; I don't understand why you didn't put a gun to my head and end this pain earlier. I know how much of a burden I have become. I feel so guilty about leaving a lifeless, cold body for you to have to identify.*

I wish I could take back all of the pain that I caused everyone, none of you deserved what I inflicted upon you day after day. I really do love you all so much. Why can't I get one moment's piece in my mind? I would give a limb for an hour of peace and quiet in my head. The worry and the guilt have slowly suffocated me until there is nothing left. I need to die. I think about it all of the time and there is no other answer but death. I haven't played my flute well in nearly two months. I miss my flute. I loved singing through it and the warm tones that we generated together. It hurts so much to think about how much of my music I have lost. I ache inside for what I used to be. I can't face my students or any of the conductors, it is all so humiliating. I hate life, I hate myself and I hate whatever is responsible for making me this sick. If I could only have my mind back. If only I could have a small piece of what used to be my reality. This agitation and panic I feel coursing through my body is unbearable. Does God think that somehow my soul will be purified if I just suffer enough? Why can't I have peace, peace, just a tiny bit of peace. That diva; why did she pick me to torment round the clock, what did I ever do to God to deserve this? At least she will die with me, her hideous concert will finally be over and the curtain will close on her forever, just what she deserves. I hate myself for talking about her like she really exists, but how in God's name am I supposed to think any other way? She tortures my mind all of the time. I can't remember what it was like to go through a day without her. Did I really have a normal life before all of this started? Is anyone going to answer me? Of course not. I need to die, I really need to die, don't I God? I hope I don't go to hell even though I deserve it. Why can't I just die in a car accident? Now I am repeating myself, nothing but the idiotic rantings of a lunatic musician. I was a musician. I was a good musician. I feel I have insulted even the paper and ink I am using with such self-pity. I disgust myself. I miss the music of our quintets at home. I will miss the warm comfort of mother's arms.

Please think kindly of me after I am gone. Please forgive me. I love all of you more than you will ever know.

The thought of escaping this existence and being free of the burden of having to live with suffocating depression, ridiculous highs, hallucinations, and the stinging omnipresent feeling of hopelessness, has driven me to a place so black and desolate, I truly believe only death will provide the relief I so desperately want.

As I close my eyes to contemplate my death performance the next day, I pray to receive the calmness of deep sleep, but I am wrong once again. Even in these final preparations I am interrupted by the dark rhythms of the Tarantella once more. As the spiders begin to emerge again from the walls, I can hear a scream, deep and violent and I realize the sound is coming from deep within me. I leap to my feet, in fear of the spiders and run for the safety of my parents' room. I am covered with these giant spiders as I enter my parent's room and shaking violently, I plead with my father in desperation to rid me of them. My father holds me tightly in his arms and talks to me reassuringly. He tells me that if he holds me tight enough that the spiders will not remain on my body. He tries to tell me that the spiders are only in my mind, but this time it does not work. As he holds me in his arms, I can faintly hear him whispering orders to my mother to call for the doctor to get help as quickly as possible. I can hear those anxious sounds of my parents, only as echoes drowned by the sound of the vicious Tarantella. I tightly close my eyes and try to hold on to reality as I wait for my deliverance.

5

My Life's Ultimate Dissonance

Suicide and the Asylum

I struggle to hear the words coming from my psychiatrist, "I am admitting you to the psychiatric intensive care unit now". My exhausted mind finds the existence of an intensive care unit for the mentally ill incredibly absurd. The notion that I need intensive care seems ludicrous to me. I look at my parents sitting stoically beside me; they had taken me, in my very altered state, directly to the hospital. I argue for a few moments with my doctor about his decision to hospitalize me, but it is half-hearted and very soon I start hearing the scratching sounds in the walls again. The hallucinations I am suffering from are distracting me and it is all I can do not to get up out of my chair and run from the room, run from the sounds of the spiders that I am convinced are clawing through the wall. I feel so ashamed that I cannot will them away. My doctor tries to tell me that the spiders are not real; that the spiders are in my mind and I am simply suffering from hallucinations, but his words are of little comfort to me. Part of me realizes that in reality the spiders are merely distorted hallucinations, a byproduct of my diseased brain, but a much bigger part of me cannot ignore the persistent and terrifying arachnids. Why can't I be logical about this and ignore the spiders? It is impossible to reconcile reality and the spiders within my fatigued mind.

My doctor asks me if I have been planning to kill myself and even though I know that I am extremely suicidal and have made elaborate plans to kill myself, I am reticent to feed him further details. Why does he need to know something so personal? He keeps up his incessant line of questioning about my suicidal intentions and rapidly tiring of the interrogation, I reach into my purse and hand him my carefully prepared notes for my planned death scene. Even as I am handing him the evidence of my suicidal intent, the ambivalence over whether to live or die is excruciating. I agree to the hospitalization and I am promptly taken to the psychiatric intensive care unit.

As I walk the long corridor from admissions to the I.C.U., I notice the doors to the unit are locked. I feel like I am being put in prison for a crime I did not commit. The people who should be in this prison are the ones who occupy my mind without permission. They should be put in their own special quiet room without windows so they can argue over a life they do not own and plans they should not be making. They are the guilty parties. They should receive the punishment, not me. I only want to take my beloved flute and make music, without their interference, without their unwanted agitation and soulless stealing of my one great treasure; my life's emotion and my ability to transfer it to others through my music.

While I am waiting to be admitted, I am put temporarily in one of the "quiet rooms" behind the nurses' station. The room is anything but quiet. In fact, it's extremely disquieting. It consists of bare walls, well scrubbed as though in need of removal of blood from former torture victims. It has a small bed in the center of the room with leather restraints hanging off of it. All the more proof that the victims who have stayed here have done so unwillingly and were forced to endure untold cruelties. The door to the room is unusually thick, as though needing reinforcement from the useless pummeling of occupants trapped within its walls. There is a tiny window in the middle of the door so that one cannot see too much of the richness of the outside world, forcing its occupant to concentrate on the vacant bareness of the inner parts of this desolate cell. I panic at the thought that I am going to be trapped in this place forever. I cannot believe my doctor is going to leave me in one of these barren, cold rooms. My desire to jump up and run out as quickly as possible increases with each passing second. As I am about to run in a desperate panic, a nurse appears and informs me that my occupancy of this room is only temporary and that once I am admitted I will be taken to my room in the unit.

The quiet rooms, I later found out, were there for patients who were "acting out" and were considered dangerous towards themselves or others. These cubicles were situated directly behind the nurses' station so that the nurses could keep a close eye on the patient in crisis. The thought of being trapped in one of those claustrophobic rooms was incomprehensible to me.

As I stand in the quiet room completely numb and spent from the psychosis and depression, I hear the nurse as though from a distance telling me in a monotone that she has to search my belongings in case I have any "sharps" (psychiatric lingo for anything that one could cut themselves with), or medications that I can use to harm myself. I tell her no, even though I know that I have a razor blade in my bag. Even while I am agreeing to hospitalization the ambivalence over whether or not to kill myself is intense, and I still want the option to kill myself if this unbearable pain does not subside. Needless to say the nurse finds the hidden razor and I am both embarrassed and angry. The nurse also insists on searching the clothes I have on, taking away what little human dignity I have left and forcing me to feel trapped like a wild animal being prepared for its zoo cage. She asks if I have anything hidden in my bra or underwear. I feel violated and less than human, as I weakly tell her no. The nurse takes several of my personal items as though bounty from a pirate expedition and claims that they may be dangerous to me or other patients in the unit. I am sure she wants those items for herself, but she tells me calmly, again in that wonderful monotone, that they will be placed at the nurses' station for safekeeping. I am told the items will be returned to me when I am discharged. Discharge is not a word I can fully comprehend at this point. I may escape, I may die within these walls, but surely I will not be discharged as though I am a medication being pushed from a syringe. I begin to picture the ways in which these nurses can aid the angry soprano and the spiders in making my life even more difficult to bear. I do not sense the warmth and comfort of nurses that one pictures at hospitals near the battlefront gently holding the hands of the soldiers fighting for their lives. I see only prison guards waiting to rap my knuckles if I do not suit their near term plans or purposes in the operation of this bizarre place.

I hear the nurse's voice speaking once again to me in that cold, impersonal manner which surely has been the result of much study; voice training perhaps in a special, sick operatic school for nurse divas. Her tone is controlled, yet sufficiently modulated to allow a touch of impatience mixed with a righteousness which could only come from those gifted performers specially anointed to serve in this ungodly place. That imperious voice is telling me that I cannot have my precious tape player and headphones—the last incremental vestiges of my life in music. It becomes clear in my clouded mind that this nurse diva realizes all too well that I can strangle myself with the sounds of Chopin and that I can choke to death on the thick joy of music created by this master who came from outside her world. It is clear to me now that my path to sanity requires not only killing the illness in my mind, but also coupling this new found diva with the angry soprano so that they can dance to the true rhythms of their insipid and empty lives. In one grand gesture this nurse diva has plucked from my life, no, from my very soul, the only respite I have left from the voices and the spiders. Chopin is the only music that provides me with any relief; I can lose myself in the lush harmonies and the poignant lyrical phrases, and if I am lucky, for a moment or two, hear more music than madness. I ask the nurse how I can possibly kill myself with a tape recorder and headphones. The idea that I could do anything to harm myself with the only instrument of music I have left is preposterous to me, and I argue vehemently that I should be allowed to keep my music. Unfortunately, it is a one-way conversation. The diva answers back to me in those vast, sonorous and yet monotonic tones that she studied so hard to perfect, that it was essential to remove these items from my person. She speaks of my person as though I am existing within some form of robotic suit which she can deal with at will and which protects her from touching my highly contaminated body, or from reaching too near the insidious insanity that covers my face like a mask of red death. She knows full well that music was not and could not be included in the curriculum of that gray lifeless school she attended and would only introduce to her unfeeling body, emotions which would cause her endless human responses for which she was obviously unprepared. In the end, her divas' diploma wins out and she deftly ends all negotiations by removing the tape recorder and headphones and unfeelingly throws them into a white plastic effects bag with my smudged and partly blotted out name on its underbelly.

I am then taken through locked doors to the medical purgatory called "THE UNIT". The unit contains a number of rooms filled with poor lost souls much like myself in various states of forgiveness, trying to attain the elevated state of grace already achieved by the diva nurses. On the way to the unit, I observe the large nurses' station, which has a counter that serves to separate the patients from the uncontaminated nurse population contained behind it. The counter supports a large glass window, which the nurses keep closed at all times. I suspect that there is a positive air pressure system so that this glass membrane can keep the nurses from having to mix their inhalations with the impurity of the mental patients. The nurses who are clearly protective of their station feel that it must be guarded against intervention from those of us who are less clean. This protection requires a great deal of activity behind the counter and I will soon learn that in my room within the unit, I can only hope to visit with the nurses where they huddled, protecting themselves from the shocking environment of the patient occupied spaces. The diva nurse motions to those other nurses, who are clearly guarding the counter, that the locked door should be tripped open so that the nurse and I can quietly enter this land of recovery.

Now I can look forward to bright conversations with the occupants within about their angry sopranos and battles fought and lost, and wait patiently for the warm comforting hand of that battle scarred nurse that I know will never come to visit. Once in the unit, the nurse locks the door behind us and I am led quietly to my room.

My room is small and contains two beds. One bed looks very comfortable and appears to be a regular hospital type bed and the other bed, which the nurse tells me is mine, consists of a box spring and mattress lying directly on the floor. This poor excuse for comfort will be my bed? I sit down on the box spring and mattress and look longingly at the regular hospital bed. The great wisdom of the diva nurse has clearly determined that purgatory for me must start here and I am denied the earthly comforts of those beings who have already achieved a finer state of grace than I. Dante would have been proud of this arrangement, however, I cannot see a path to greater glory other than near term occupation of the regular hospital bed. On the other side of my room, there are two desks, side by side, with no writing implements and one empty drawer each. The drawers do not matter in that I have nothing to store in them and writing utensils are clearly for those mindless souls gifted enough to write their story in their own blood. I particularly like the omnipresent smell of old hospital food, which adds to the sense of purgatory. Although it does not have the acrid odor of brimstone, it does have a distinctive stale component, which I later discover can be attributed to the inappropriate aging of the food in the inner recesses of the dungeon they call the food preparation area.

Standing in my stark empty room, I suddenly feel a hollow pang of loneliness. After the nurse gives me a short tour of my room, she hurries back behind the protective glass of the nurses' station. Are we really that frightening to be around? I place what little belongings I have left with me on my bed. I turn to look out the window of my room and for a moment feel protected from the spiders. Surely they cannot get me here, but my feeling of safety is fleeting. After just minutes in my room, I hear the spiders in the walls scratching at the plaster in a concerted attempt to get through them and attack me. How could they have found me so quickly? My mind is tired and wracked with unreal sights and sounds manufactured by my brain. It is an immense struggle trying to weed through the tangled input. What is real and what is not has melded together and I feel like my brain is flailing about in the thick atmosphere of my tortured reality. It is an exhausting effort trying to decipher the messages my brain is sending to me. On the one hand I have been told that the spiders are a by–product of my illness and therefore not real, but on the other hand I have omnipresent doubt that perhaps my doctor is wrong about the spiders being just an illusion, perhaps they are real and I am in true danger.

I run from the spiders in my room into the dining room, where later I am told meals are served and group therapy is held. The room is fairly stark with a couple of tables, a couch and a few chairs, with a television in the far corner. The television is turned on and I can hear faintly through the screeching din of the sounds in my head, a religious program telling its viewers to "repent or be sent to hell". In front of the television sits an elderly woman who appears to be around eighty years old, watching with intense interest, seemingly oblivious to her surroundings. There is a male patient, much younger and quite thin, who is alternately standing up and sitting down in one of the chairs opposite the elderly woman, while loudly yelling, "I never get to watch the shows I like because the old woman always watches the religious channel". No one seems to hear the young man's ranting, including the elderly woman, who on occasion, without looking away from the television screen, yells epithets back at the agitated young man. The young man appears doubly helpless because neither the nurses, nor the elderly woman (clutching the remote control tightly in her hand), seem to listen to his cries for relief. This almost appears to be a classic "Punch and Judy" show without the closed curtains and proscenium arch to separate them from the reality of the rest of the room. The only thing lacking is a large club in each of the antagonist's hands. I am actually thankful for the "show" and sit down on the couch, trying to focus my attention on the people in the room, rather than on the atrocious duet in my mind between singer and spider.

This place, I will call "The Vistas of Heaven", is known to me by its reputation for calm surroundings and a clean environment. Needless to say, the figures of the furniture, dirty and distorted, appear to have come from a painting by Salvador Dali and in true surrealist mode, the cushions that should be soft are hard, the legs that should be stiff and straight are curved and soft in their appearance, as though they have half melted from some past fire and were left in place for those of us that could sit on such distorted platforms. The occupants of the unit, or the "unclean", had left messages to their God in the form of graffiti on these misshapen couches. The words were formed with what appeared to be old grape juice. I guess they had run out of ink from the empty pots that sat on their empty desks. As with the finger of destiny, the patients had writ with their fingers and as from an Omar Khayyam tale having writ their message, moved on.

I wonder why the couch has not been cleaned of its great prophecy. It seems to fit somehow with the Punch and Judy show and the bizarre thirties atmosphere. The pre–war Germans could have done much to caricature the look and mood of this seemingly transported scene. This scene out of a Dadaist painting, lacks only the machine guns of the faithful to make sure that the religious program gets changed. On the left side of the room there is a large picture window through which I can see the nurses' station. They are still busily protecting their part of the institution's turf while convincing themselves that they are saner than the occupants within. I notice a nurse staring at me through the glass and I suddenly feel very naked and exposed. I try very hard to refrain from any handstands, summersaults or club wielding that might injure her glare and force her to inspect me more carefully. I don't appreciate this kind of admiration; she is not watching me for my music but rather for my madness. Now I perform for a totally different audience, filled with critics all analyzing my every move, anticipating the many wrong notes yet to be played in their clinical theater. Feeling like I am on display upsets me and my immediate thought is to get off this nightmarish stage and go home, but there is no turning back, I have shared my darkest secrets with my doctor, which includes my intense desire to die. I have voluntarily committed myself, but I also know if I ask to leave in my present condition my doctor will not allow it. I'm not sure when I will get out.

On the other side of the dining room is a glass door that leads to a small outdoor patio. I am feeling claustrophobic in this room and quickly walk over to explore the small enclosure. The patio is enclosed and has very high walls. I appreciate the fresh air, a welcome change from the stale smells of the unit. I can still hear the spiders scratching at the walls, but I feel a modicum of additional safety on the patio because its walls are made of concrete. Surely the spiders will not be able to get through the unbreakable material. The patio is perhaps five paces wide, and I find myself pacing the small area, trying as hard as I can, not to panic. I have learned from many years of suffering with panic attacks, that the worst thing I can do is let the panic get the best of me. Once I allow that first wave of panic to spill over the internal wall I have spent months building up, brick by brick, I will be in the throws of a major panic attack, the flood gates will open and mind numbing terror will engulf my body. I tell myself I must stay as calm as possible, a panic attack is the last thing I need in my current situation. I try employing a mind trick I play with myself whenever I feel a panic attack coming on. I pretend that I am just about to go out on stage and perform a difficult concerto. To many this image would create an even greater feeling of panic, but to me, anxiety and the concert stage go hand in hand, and as a concert soloist I never have the luxury of falling apart before or during a performance. No matter how much anxiety I feel, the show has to go on. So, when panic strikes, I simply turn down the anxiety level from Fortissimo to Pianissimo, and the panic lies dormant for the next thirty minutes while I play. I distract myself from the panic by getting lost in the art of making music, caressing phrases just so, playing with a warm tone and concentrating on interpretation and ensemble. It was only after a concert that I allowed myself the luxury of falling apart. As usual, this imagery helps me get through the icy twinges of panic that threaten to send me over the edge entirely.

My doctor has assured me that I will be safe in the hospital and I cling to those words like a life raft in an angry ocean. As I stand in the center of the patio, I look up at the sky and am surprised to see metal bars that form a barrier across the top of the patio walls. I assume they are there to keep the patients in, but more importantly, I take comfort in the thought that the bars will keep the spiders out.

The nurse that had taken me to my room finds me out on the patio and asks me if I would like a tour of the unit. I am reeling from the sounds in my head and fighting back the panic is utterly exhausting. I say, "Yes, I would like a tour", even though I do not care to see the rest of this penitentiary, I am thankful for some company, even for just a few minutes. The nurse walks breezily down the one and only hallway in the unit, showing me the rest of the patient's rooms and a therapy room at the end of the hall. She asks me a question here and there, but I am so absorbed with quelling the panic that I am unable to answer. Down the long hallway, at the opposite end of the nurses' station, is an emergency exit. I am instructed not to try and open the door since that would activate the alarm system. I think to myself, this truly is a prison. Why can't I just snap out of it and have my mind back whole and healthy? It seems cruelly unfair and unjust. I long for the music of my tape player. I hate the nurse for taking it from me, but say nothing, for fear she will lock me away in one of those horrible quiet rooms with their ominous leather restraints and promise of dark things to come.

I am taken back to the dining room and I stand by as the nurse reaches into her pocket and like a warden, removes a large key chain. She fondles the keys, as they are her power. She handles them with control, yet with the ease of a jailer sending me back to my cell. She unlocks the door connecting the nurses' station to the unit, while I stand outside the dining room, which is well within the patients' quarters. I am alone again.

As soon as the nurse leaves me, my panic begins welling up inside me and my instinct is to flee. But flee to where? My parents had been sent home after my admission. I think about calling my family. Surely they will come and get me and take me home, but I am too ashamed to call them; ashamed that I have not been stronger, that I have not fought hard enough to overcome the demons in my head, ashamed that I want to give up and die. My intense love for my family cannot overpower my desire to be free of the spiders and the angry soprano in my head. I believe death is the only cure for my illness. How can I make them understand the pain and torment I feel? Just existing has become such a painful chore. If only they could see that my existence has turned to subsistence and there is no point in prolonging a life filled with so much anger and pain. How can I make them understand that?

I dread making the phone call, which seems all the more difficult because there is no phone in my room. Phones are considered a possible means of suicide and therefore are not allowed. For a moment I think about just how one could kill themselves with a phone, and realize the necessity of their absence from the patients' rooms. I resent not having a means of private communication with my family. The only phone contact allowed with the outside world is through an old pay phone a few feet away from the nurses' station and it affords the patients absolutely no privacy. Everyone in the unit and in the nurses' station hears everything that is said on the phone. I pace the unit hallway for over an hour building up the courage to call my family, all the while I can hear the scratching in the walls and the angry soprano commenting on what a pathetic loser I am.

I finally resolve to call home. Hesitatingly, I pick up the phone receiver and dial and after one ring my father answers the phone. I listen, my whole body shaking, to my father as he gently asks how I am. I immediately start to sob and keep apologizing over and over for disappointing him and letting down the family. He tells me that he just wants me to get well and if I need anything to call him. He then asks if

I want to speak with my mom. I say yes, even though I am having a hard time hearing because the spiders are now gnawing at the wall next to me with a vengeance, and the angry soprano is back for yet another deafening encore. I pretend to hear every word and say very little. Each member of my family in succession gets on the phone and wishes me well, but I feel there is a cold void between us and there are more pregnant pauses than words spoken. I ask that they please bring me some pajamas and some comfortable casual clothes, since all I came in with are the clothes on my back and my purse. My mother says someone will be bringing me the necessary items very soon. I apologize again profusely for hurting them and hang up the phone.

I feel terrible; none of the kind words from my family are a comfort to me. I feel more alone than I have ever felt in my entire existence. I do not know how much farther I can sink into the despair that fills my body. I need to find my mind's floor where I can rest and resume the fight I am having with the creatures that delude me.

I go back to my room and curl up in a ball on my bed and I cry until I am exhausted. A few hours later, a nurse shows up in my doorway to let me know that dinner is being served in the dining room and I should, "Get up and come and eat". I am not hungry but I go anyway, I don't want the nurse to get angry with me, and I need to be with people, any distraction from the hallucinations and depression is welcome.

Dinner is a bold adventure at The Vistas of Heaven. The dining room is filled with the odors of foods of many types; the only problem is that they are the smells that one has when one puts stale steamy food in a warmer far beyond its trial membership period. The steam used to keep the food warm is beginning to decompose the meat and the potatoes have lost their resemblance to root vegetables from the ground. The carrots appear to be bizarrely curled and split down the center with slight oozing bits of gravy protruding from their cracked lips. The chicken has been roasted at one time, but after this extensive steaming, appears much like one of my delusions with the skin hanging off the bones and its shapelessness bears little resemblance to poultry. All in all, this is food fit for someone other than me. It appears as though it has been in the inner tomb of some great Egyptian king, where it has been cooked originally as a sacrifice, but has been given many years to attain its present state after the kings dead body has already fully decomposed. Unfortunately the food lacks the preservatives given to the king's mummified body, which kept the king's shape while the food decayed. As though having just opened the inner sanctum of the tomb of King Tut, I can hardly stand the smell. I am left without even a small golden chariot from the tomb to counter balance my unfulfilled hunger. I am seriously considering going back to my room to retreat from the foul stench, but a nurse I have not had the displeasure of meeting yet, motions for me to sit on the couch. As I sit down, the nurse drops my meal tray down on the table in front of me with considerable force; smells and all. Clearly this nurse takes her meals elsewhere and is unaware of the palpable response of my olfactory senses to the food placed before me. I knew that hospital food was notorious for tasting bad, but this food should receive a gold medal for its creation of new odor combinations, and the design of undreamed of mixtures of tastes.

As I lift the cover off the tray, I see the most amazing sight of my stay in this "Vista of Heaven". It is a large piece of chicken that requires a knife in order to cut it up into bite size pieces and I have only been given a fork and a spoon. The knife is conspicuously missing. I suppress a gag as the odor from this apparent food substitute wafts to my nose. I look at the over cooked, misshapen, over steamed, rotting carcass of what used to be a portion of chicken, and poke it gingerly with my fork. Even though it appears to be disassembling before my eyes as though it has been freshly exhumed, it is so tough that the tines of my fork have a difficult time piercing the outer layers. How can I possibly cut this up without a knife? I ask the nurse why I cannot have even a tiny plastic knife, especially since she is supervising my meal. She states, in her most sonorous monotonic diva school voice, that even plastic knives are considered "sharps" and I will just have to "make do". She clearly has never tried this chicken. I cannot believe she would deny me even a plastic knife. I curse myself for being so open with my doctor. What an idiot I was. I could have been dead by now, my troubles over. Now I can't even cut up an over–cooked piece of poultry. I stab the piece of chicken with my fork and bring the entire brown mass to my lips, ripping at the meat like a cave woman. As I brave the chicken, every taste bud my tongue possesses revolts in protest. I am not the only person to complain about the food. Almost everyone in the room has something to say about how repulsive the food is. I try desperately to focus on the steady stream of complaints coming from my fellow inpatients. It takes my mind off of my own inner torment and for a few precious seconds I am numb to my inner senses.

During dinner, I am able to formally meet some of the patients. They are from all walks of life, and the vast majority of them are attempted suicides. I meet a patient who is a registered nurse by profession and she tells me her name is Susan. She is very quiet and extremely polite. Her husband is by her side, almost clinging to her in an attempt to protect her from whatever unseen forces had driven his wife to such an act of desperation. I can see a rather small bandage on the inside of her left arm. Later on she tells me that she had cut an artery. I feel such great pity for her, probably because right now it takes less effort to feel sorry for her than for myself. She has the kind of facial expression that is born out of unendurable mental anguish. I know the look. I wear it myself.

After introducing herself, Susan quickly leaves the dining room with her husband. While the nurse monitors our meal, she is cheerily trying to get us to "try and eat something" and I lean back on the couch, to distance myself from the foods' foul smell. As dinner progresses, the angry soprano continues her litany of admonitions, "Get your ass off the couch, eat the food, it tastes better than you look. Jump through the nurses window, they need the company. Take the fork and stick it in your gut. You still can't play worth a damn. Don't make excuses about the food, your playing stinks worse than it does". Her insults stab my mind like big needle pricks, and I am sure I see a spider leg reaching out, twitching, trying to grasp me from behind the television set. With panic welling within me, I ask if I can go back to my room, but the nurse forcefully tells me that I must stay a while longer and at least "attempt to eat some of my dinner". Why can't she understand that I have to get out of this room now? I am under attack. Doesn't she care? I stay seated, even though my mind is quickly filling with a sickening nervousness. I don't want my innkeepers to be upset with me, so I pick up my fork in an attempt to give the illusion that I am trying to eat.

Soon the nurse focuses her attention on another patient without a knife, desperately stabbing at the corpse of his chicken remains. I am left alone to concentrate on the rest of the room. There are six other patients in the unit besides Susan and myself, and I begin to occupy my mind by playing, "guess the affliction", anything that will throw the evil spiders and the ranting diva back into the dark recesses of their imaginary theater. I look at each patient and try to guess what they are "in for". It isn't very hard to spot the people in for depression. They have huge dark circles under their eyes and have a listlessness to them that makes them appear smaller than their actual size. The collective grief in the room is almost palpable. Funeral wakes are witness to less sadness. My heart goes out to them, but I can do nothing to make them feel better, I can't even help myself.

In the corner of the dining room is a girl named Mary. She is a very lovely woman with unusually long dark hair. She is well kempt and has big brown eyes that abruptly match my stare. For a moment it seems she knows the game I am playing. Can she tell what my "affliction" is too, just by looking at me? Can she hear the soprano in my head? Can she hear the scratching? We play the game together for a few seconds more before she goes back to picking at the cold substances on her dinner tray. What is wrong with Mary? She does not strike me as someone who suffers from depression, and she certainly doesn't seem manic. I decide Mary will require more study, a project for the evening, something to keep my mind off of the jet–black spider army that will inevitably come for me tonight. Thank God for distractions.

I move the food around on my dinner plate to make it appear that I have eaten something, an old trick from childhood. I ask to go to my room again. The nurse inspects my tray with suspicion. I tell her I simply cannot eat another bite and begin to exit the room. She starts to say something but I keep right on walking. I am relieved that she does not decide to pursue the matter further and I quickly make my retreat.

The air is decidedly fresher in my room with only the faintest smell of "dinner" clinging to my clothes. As soon as I sit down on my bed I regret leaving the dining room. The scratching in the walls is intense, and within a minute I am driven into the relative safety of the brightly lit hallway. I feel another deep twinge of loneliness as I survey the empty corridor. What am I going to do for the rest of the night without the comforting tones of my Chopin? How I loathe the nurse for taking my only vestige of peace from me. In desperation, I begin to hum Chopin in my mind, trying to block the hollow scraping sounds out by re–creating, note by note, the lovely melody that begins the second movement of the piano concerto. For a few minutes I stand against the wall in the hallway with my eyes closed, focusing on the only piece of music that has brought me any comfort over the past six months. I have memorized every note, every dynamic change, and every entrance of every solo. I know every melodic line of every instrument, and can feel the glorious ensemble as each sensitively played melody is passed from one solo instrument to the next with lyrical precision. I can hear the soloist's entrance. The exquisite touch imbued with a passion that can only be communicated when composer and artist have become one. My concentration is abruptly broken around the thirtieth bar. She is back, the selfish singer, throwing a tantrum. How dare I push her off stage. How could I give away the spotlight to some wretched piano concerto? The angry soprano starts in with her usual litany of profanities and I slowly sink to the floor in a state of despair and hopelessness I had not thought possible.

I feel a sharp tapping on my shoulder. I can feel black pointy legs, stabbing at my shoulder. Soon I will feel their fangs sinking into my arm. I leap up off of the floor and spin around to face them, ready to fight to the death, but there are no spiders. I am disoriented and confused, where did they go? It takes me a few seconds to realize that there are no spiders. The touch I have interpreted as being so deadly is really that of a unit nurse. She is standing in front of me with her hands on her hips. She has found me in a heap on the hallway floor sobbing and asks if I am all right. I still have all that adrenalin pumping through my system; my body is prepared for a fight to the death, not a nurse with an intrusive jab. I scream at her never to sneak up on me again. How dare she creep up behind me and purposely try to scare me like that. Unlike my other inmates, she did not have to "guess my affliction". She knew exactly what I is "in for" and should know better. The nurse looks at me with a patronizing smile, and tells me to, "Calm down, it will be alright" as she leads me back to the dining room; back to the foul smells of dinner.

As I walk back into the dining room I get a much-needed laugh. There are five patients still braving their dinners; boldly sawing away at their respective pieces of chicken with their forks stabbed into the meat to hold it steady, while they cut away at the tough lumps of flesh with the sides of their spoons. I don't know who came up with the idea first, but one of them has discovered that the edges of the "harmless" spoons are actually quite sharp and soon everyone is trying this exotic new cutting tool. Each patient has his or her own unique way of utilizing this new slicing implement. Some are using the front edge of the spoon sawing with short, quick efficiency and others prefer the long edge of the spoon, employing a longer yet more intense cutting stroke. Necessity truly is the mother of invention, even in a mental institution. I feel like cheering. The score is now patients–one, chicken–zero. We have beaten their "no knives" policy and I feel a rush of empowerment, a tiny victory for the "inmates".

To appease the nurse I stay in the dining room for a few minutes, watching with admiration as each piece of chicken is drawn and quartered. Once I feel it is safe, I make a hasty retreat back out into the hallway. The air out in the hallway is a noticeable improvement from the clingy odor of stale food still present in the dining area. I walk back to my room and sit down on my bed. I am exhausted from the events of the day and my limbs move sluggishly as I dig in my bag for something to wear to bed. I have nothing and it is getting late. I decide I am too tired to give a damn and lay back and fall asleep with my shoes still on.

From my bed, I can't tell where that bright light shining on my face is coming from, but I know I don't like it. Awakened out of a dead sleep, I quickly sit up and try to make sense of this insulting illumination. I feel like I am being hunted. It reminds me of a symphonic poem by Cesar Frank called The Accursed Huntsman. The poem depicts a huntsman who goes hunting on Sunday instead of attending church and as his punishment he is bewitched and plagued by hideous demons. Is God punishing me also? As I begin to speak, I hear the unmistakable sound of leather that has not yet been broken in, like the squeak of a brand new leather saddle being put through its paces on a long horseback ride, but I'm not on the trail tonight. That I know for certain. The light is coming towards me at an alarming rate and now I can make out the faint outline of a nurse walking towards my bed. I ask her what she wants and state that I am sleeping. She replies in a matter of fact tone of voice, "Bed check". I couldn't believe she would wake me up, knowing how bone tired I am. How could she do that? This is the second time in a row the nursing staff has upset me, and I am outraged at their callous indifference to my suffering. Little did I know she would be back with that irritating flashlight approximately every fifteen minutes throughout the night to make sure I was not trying to kill myself.

I have often wondered why the interval is every fifteen minutes; surely it is possible to do all the damage needed to kill myself in twelve minutes. It might even take me 14.5 minutes, but I would still beat the interval between checks and the nurse would have lost this game of "catch me if you can". Why don't they have a nurse at my bedside holding my hand, to give me the strength to triumph over the night? Did the nurse wait at the nurses' station counting down on a large clock, saying to her compatriots, "I don't think she can do it in twelve minutes, so we probably have time for that coffee you brought". Or, in the alternate, these nurses might be waging dollar bets to see if I will survive the given fifteen minute break, or whether they will find me in the midst of hanging myself and lose to the mental bookie who stays behind the counter. I wonder who the Nobel Prize winning genius is, who after much probabilistic analysis, determined that it would take more than a three sigma variation from the mean, for a patient to kill themselves in less than fifteen minutes, therefore saving the nurse on watch extra steps to each bedside, to make sure that every mental "sickie" had not had sufficient time to kill herself.

That's what it must have been, a special work measurement engineer, hired by those great psychiatrists that I have known, who could analyze all of the steps and variations on all the themes that were possible for my miserable hands and feet, in order to accomplish this dire task in less than fifteen minutes. I can see the report now, sitting on the diva nurse's desk, open to the section on special work elements combining a hand twist with a thumb maneuver, which would allow my poor body to become lifeless under those special movements in less than fifteen minutes. Think of the staff reductions that were possible with this analysis. Think of the nurses looking for other work in alternate industries because they weren't needed to do the twelve–minute bed check because it actually took more than fifteen minutes to complete the deed—all detailed in the standard five hundred–page manual of bed check procedures. The manual must really be accurate because nobody killed themselves while I was in the facility and there is no sign that they had to hire extra bed check nurses. The insights and the marvels of modern science being applied to a psychiatric ward give me great comfort. In fact, in combination with the rubber chicken, it gives me a complete sense of safety and faith in the hands of those who are dealing with my fragile mind.

After my rather thorough analysis of the bed check situation I realize that The Vistas of Heaven is the place to be for those of us who were lacking in all of the amenities of life in the real world. In fact, when I first saw the entrance to this hospital, I thought it looked grand and pastoral, more like a park than a mental institution, complete with a lovely portico covered with green ivy. There were even sweet brown jackrabbits and timid deer eating quietly from the lovely carpet of luxuriant green lawn in front of the hospital. Only now do I realize what a clever façade those warped engineers had constructed, to make this place look like the witches' house in Hansel and Gretel, leading the innocent patients to believe that delicious treats await them inside. I did not see the partially covered sign with the bright words exposed under the green ivy, "Contents may be hazardous to your health!"

The next day, my sister Wendy and her husband Tom come to visit me. I feel extremely self-conscious in front of Tom. I sense that he is uncomfortable in this strange place. He keeps touching Wendy as though to keep her from being exposed to a virulent disease. He looks at his watch and then at Wendy and then at me and follows the nurses with his eyes as they move back and forth behind us. I know that there is nothing I can possibly say that will make them feel better about this grim situation, so I quickly wrap up the conversation and tell them that they should get back on the road before it gets to be too late. Wendy's husband quickly agrees. As Wendy glances furtively at me, she tentatively reaches one hand towards mine, but her husband already has his arm firmly around her waist and is moving her rapidly down the hall. At the locked unit door we hug briefly and Wendy quickly turns away and begins to walk out the door with her husband clutching her waist tightly. I wish as hard as I can at this moment for the life we once shared as children, hopping up and down on our beds together and sharing our "secret plans" for the holidays. I watch through the small glass window of the locked I.C.U. door, as my sister leans her head against her husband's shoulder, walking slowly out into the night. I have failed her yet again. I am no longer the big sister who always looks out for her, now she is taking care of me and I don't like this shaky role reversal. I go back to my room and cry myself to sleep.

I didn't sleep very well that night, the suicide watch continued as before, orderly and on time. Prisoners in Alcatraz were afforded more privacy. I was now living in a fish bowl, with my every movement monitored and recorded in my chart. To make matters worse, they kept the bathroom doors locked. Every time I had to use the restroom I had to ask a nurse to come and open it for me. She would return a few minutes later and lock it again. The sound of keys clinking together became an all too familiar precursor to everything from bodily functions to drawing with crayola crayons, (the I.C.U.'s writing implement of choice).

Each morning in the unit is more depressing than the day before, and I am getting increasingly claustrophobic in this tiny locked unit. I can smell the all too familiar smell of cadaverine that is referred to by the straight-faced nurses as our food, which once again has been sitting around entirely too long behind the nurses' station. I fully expected to see early this morning, six or eight vultures drying their wings behind the nurses' station, waiting to gain access to the food when no one is looking. Breakfast is its own adventure; it is definitely different than dinner in that it is served in the morning. The oatmeal, the standard of the meal, has the texture of crushed bricks and the toast is served on a bed of warm water, which gives it a wet, chewy texture and tastes somewhat like the oatmeal, except it is a different shade of brown. Along with this glorious beginning of the day, I am given a handful of pills to swallow. They actually have approximately the same lumpiness as the oatmeal. I notice that there are a lot more pills in my hand than I normally take each morning at home. I ask the nurse to please tell me what I am taking and how much. This nurse is unfortunately the diva and she tells me slowly and in that monotone I am beginning to hate, that my doctor will explain to me after breakfast the complexities and medical nuances of this rainbow array of pills. Not wanting to upset things, I swallow them all in one gulp. She thanks me, like a trainer thanks its seal for a trick well executed and moves on to her next target. I know full well that my question at best is rhetorical, in that she cannot explain to me the intricacies of this mélange of potions in pill form, anymore than she can tell me how many feedback circuits I have in my visual pathway, or the use of tyrosine hydroxylase in the acceleration of my mental processes. I know she could make my bed without legs and she can find the right place to crease the sheet and I know she can serve rubber chicken on a soggy tray, but she cannot explain why I take the particular mixture of pills that she feeds me each day and she certainly does not know how to keep the angry soprano quiet. She cannot even grasp my hand warmly and wish me sweet dreams and tuck me into bed.

It is not long after breakfast that the scratching starts up again in earnest. No matter where I go in the unit I hear the spiders, scratching and gnawing at the walls, accompanied by the angry soprano. I am surprised at my singing diva. It is not often that she allows something else in my mind to share her spotlight, but today she seems happy to let the spiders take center stage. I am sure she will make up for it later with some ear shattering encores. I pace the hallway for some time until going back into my room. Somehow the noises seem fainter in my room, so I shut the door. I cannot have been more wrong. As soon as I shut the door I can see them everywhere. The floor is covered with spiders. I scream and jump up onto the top of my desk. I am now moving beyond rational thought and the spiders' world is quickly devouring any sense I have of reality. I cannot believe that my doctor has not protected me from them, all of his promises are lies and now I am going to get bitten. My mind begins to warp from the fear and distorts everything. As I look down at the carpet, its patterns seem to melt into each other creating whole new geometries. The air pressure in the room feels different, somehow increased, adding a tense thickness to the air. The feelings of safety and security my doctor promised to me are gone. Everything is spinning and I begin to scream. I cannot endure even one more Tarantella. Thankfully, two nurses hear my screams and come running into my room. One nurse puts her arms around me and the other stands at my side, telling me repeatedly that there are no spiders. I want desperately to believe her but my eyes tell a very different tale. I bury my face in the nurse's arms and hold on to her for dear life. The noises from the cruelly tenacious creatures are deafening, and they are becoming louder and even more intense. I struggle not to cry as I continue to cling with all my might to my human life raft. I am now drenched in sweat, and the nurses cannot get me to leave my room. I am paralyzed with terror. I watch as the spiders swarm around the nurses' feet. Why don't the nurses run? After a few minutes, the sounds of the spiders mercifully start to subside and I can no longer hear the sounds of their hollow legs on the walls, scurrying away from me at top speed as they go back into their jagged black holes to hide in the dead space of the walls.

I cry for the rest of the morning. There is nothing that can protect me from their black presence. I am given a shot ordered by my doctor shortly after the incident. I sleep until early evening, blissfully ignorant of the spiders, the soprano, and the depression.

With the added drugs, the days in the unit melt one into the other. The number of pills I am given each morning increases and I often forget what day it is or how much time has passed since I have spoken with a fellow patient. The medication dulls my senses to the outside world, as well as to my mind's stage, but it at least gives me a short respite from the psychosis.

I wake early one morning and discover that a very nice older woman has been admitted to the unit. Her name is Kate and she suffers from severe depression, but despite her suicidal tendencies she is a real firebrand. It seems she lives to buck the system. She hates the I.C.U. and constantly talks about "getting over to the other side". The "other side" is the part of the hospital that is unlocked. Often patients will come into the I.C.U. for stabilization then are transferred to the unlocked unit when they are better. Some of us stay longer than others. All of us in the I.C.U. are tortured daily with picturesque views of a wonderfully huge lawn from our rooms; the lawn none of us are allowed to enjoy. The I.C.U. patients never see a single blade of grass because we are never allowed outside. I watch by the hour as patients on the unlocked ward walk out on the soft green grass whenever the mood strikes them. There are no fences or locked doors on the "other side"—they are free. I long to be outside even for just a few minutes, but in my present state my doctor will not allow it.

My parents have been visiting me often since I was admitted and each time they try to be as bright and cheery as possible. When they come to visit, I try to pretend I am somehow being miraculously cured. We each compose our own very special character pieces for each other and we always carefully design them to express a happy mood. Of course not one of us is giving a very believable performance. There is too much pain. Every time we conclude a visit I can see in their eyes such a profound sadness. I wish I could just hop in the car and go home with them, but my doctor won't allow it. My family does, however, convince my doctor, on occasion, to let me out to eat lunch with them. It is the only time I have anything decent to eat. As I sit with my family, out under the trees in front of the main building of the hospital, I revel in the fresh air. I keep re–playing in my head the opening flute solo from Claude Debussy's symphonic poem, The Afternoon of a Faun. The visions conjured up by the sensitive harmonies of this impressionist work combine with the warmth of the midday sun to relax me. I forget for a while about the bad smells, beat up old furniture, the lack of privacy and the close quarters of the I.C.U.

As part of our therapy, all the patients are required to attend group therapy sessions. They are held in the dining room, which also serves as a multi–purpose room. The group therapy sessions are virtually the only activity offered in the I.C.U.. Each day we are rounded up before the session by the nursing staff. One by one we are dragged from our rooms in protest; none of us wants to be yanked from our melancholic ruminations and isolation. Today is no different and for the next hour I sit half asleep in a drug–induced haze listening to other patients' tales of pain. The therapist conducting group therapy is obnoxiously cheery and his demeanor grates on me like a sour note played indifferently in the middle of a fragile melodic tune.

The therapist always starts the sessions by telling the group "whatever is said during these sessions stays here". No one in the group is to ever break confidentiality for any reason, so that way people can feel safe to bare their souls, without having to worry about repercussions at their place of employment or in their personal lives. We make a silent promise of confidentiality to each other and begin the session. I am wary of the notion that it is o.k. to share my innermost emotions with a relative stranger, but that is what we are all encouraged to do. The therapy sessions help bring our tiny foster family together and cultivate a deeper appreciation of each person's inner agonies. Looking around the circle of patients, I quietly survey the group. We are quite a disheveled looking assembly. A lot of us are so depressed that we can't even comb our hair in the morning and we all seem to be wearing the same old workout clothes; the I.C.U.'s special uniform. We look like a big collection of rag dolls, in all stages and manner of decay, but the therapist continually reminds us that despite our state of dilapidation, we are still amongst the living and we have to learn how to make the best of it. During our hour–long sessions we create a mighty ensemble of anguish. As soloists, our disorders make sad, demented melodies, but when combined, our disorders create a great symphony of pain.

Out of all of the group therapy sessions, I enjoy Art Therapy the most. It is the only group where music is played and I always put in my requests early. The hospital does not have a music therapist, so this is as close as I ever get to music as a therapeutic tool. I enjoy drawing and sculpting while listening to the music. It is a nice change of pace and the art therapist always asks what types of projects we would like to work on and makes every effort to get the appropriate supplies. While I do take pleasure in art therapy, I have to admit that I came to enjoy it for an entirely different reason. I enjoyd poking fun at the therapist who has a spacey quality to her voice, which simply fuels the prankster in me. I find her very hard to take seriously as she goes around the table analyzing each patients' newly completed drawings. We are often asked to create a drawing that reflects how we feel at the present time. I simply draw the silliest thing I can think of just to see what ridiculous analysis she will come up with. One day towards the end of my hospitalization, I took a yellow marker and drew a simple drawing of a banana, and after the therapist had analyzed her own drawing, which was admittedly quite imaginative, she moved on to my all important "banana" picture. I could hardly keep a straight face while she spent a full ten minutes analyzing my yellow banana. She felt the banana held great significance for me and stated that obviously I was not feeling very open today since I had chosen the banana, a fruit with a very "thick skin". She went on to say that she thought the yellow color was a "Happy color" which is "Nice to see". She held up the picture of the banana for the rest of the group to study while pointing at specific parts of the banana for dramatic emphasis. She then went on to tell me that because I drew a banana that is obviously "Ripe, yet still unpeeled", I was obviously not ready to share my innermost feelings with the others in the group. She went on with her pithy analogies by saying that I was not ready to "Peel back my thick banana skin yet and expose my deepest concerns". She asked me several questions about what I thought the texture of the peel was like and if the banana was part of a larger bunch that I had subconsciously forgotten to draw. At this point I was biting the inside of my mouth not to laugh and the rest of the group seemed on the verge of a laughing fit themselves, but somehow we all managed to maintain a straight face out of respect for the therapist who obviously meant well. For me, art therapy was therapeutic–just not in the way it was intended. The laughs I derived from poking fun at the therapist were invaluable to me, so I guess it did serve its purpose after all and looking back on it perhaps the therapist knew what I needed all along.

Each day my doctor visits me in the morning, usually after breakfast. We talk about everything from the weather to how I slept. Everyday I beg to be moved to the freedom of the unlocked unit. He tells me "I am not ready yet". I hate hearing those words. One day, out of the blue, my doctor decides to walk me over to the main building to have our session in his office. I cannot believe my luck. I try to walk as slowly as possible, inhaling the delicious fresh air. It is heaven. I haven't been outside in what seems like eons and the sun's warmth on my face is sheer bliss. All too soon we arrive at the door to the main building, and I am once again under the harsh artificial lights. The couch in his office is extremely comfortable, much better than the beat up furniture in the I.C.U. Between the softness of the couch and my morning medications I am feeling quite drowsy and am having a hard time understanding his questions. I don't really care what he asks me, I am out of the unit, free, even if it is just for an hour.

Unfortunately my freedom will not even last a full twenty minutes. It seems no matter how much medication I am given; the spiders are immune to their effects. After about ten minutes in my doctor's office, I start to hear the all too familiar scratching sounds coming from inside the walls. I keep asking my doctor if he hears anything, and he says no. He tries to continue the session, but I can no longer focus on his questions. All I can hear is the plaster falling in chunks onto the floor as the spiders burrow their way into the room. I ask more and more emphatically if he can hear them. He tries to reassure me that there is nothing to hear. I pull my feet up onto the couch in anticipation of their entrance. I ask once more if he can hear them. All I can see are his lips moving more emphatically. I hear nothing, just the scratching of the spiders. I cover my eyes and start to panic. I feel myself being pulled off of the couch. My doctor then puts his arm around me and starts to walk me back to the unit. The intensity of the sounds is increasing and by the time we reach the hallway leading to the I.C.U. I am seeing them everywhere. I begin to bat at them with my arms and try to kick them away with my legs. I am in a total frenzy by the time I get back to my room.

Before long, a nurse comes into my room and asks me to come with her. I get up and she puts one arm over my shoulder and slowly walks me to the nurses' station as I continue to bat at my black nemeses while crying hysterically. She unlocks the unit door leading directly into the nurses' station. Once inside, I see my doctor talking in low tones to one of the nurse's as I am led past him. I beg my doctor not to place me in one of the awful, dark quiet rooms, but he simply looks away from me, indifferent to my panic. He has ordered me placed in one of the "quiet rooms" and there they give me a shot of Ativan to help calm me down. The shot I don't mind, but being placed in one of the quiet rooms I do mind. Why is my doctor being so cruel to me? I remember the quiet rooms from my admission and over time have seen violent, manic and profoundly psychotic patients placed in them for varying amounts of time. I always felt pity for them, being locked in one of those tiny rooms. The quiet rooms are the ultimate cages. I only vaguely remember what the quiet room looks like on the inside from my short visit during my admission and it is worse than I remember. The room has hard concrete floors and in the middle of the room there is a bed attached to the floor with several leather restraints hanging off both sides. I am led to the bed and asked to lie down; to my intense relief they do not utilize the restraints. I lie down and the nurse gives me the injection, then she unceremoniously leaves the room and shuts and locks the door behind her. I start to cry in a loud staccato. As the Ativan begins to take effect, the spiders start to retreat and my fear lessens as I fall into a fitful sleep.

After a few hours I am awakened by the sound of the door to my quiet room being opened. A nurse comes in and tells me I can go back into the unit. My relief is intense as I am led out of the room and back into the dining area. I am so relieved to be out of that room that I hug the nurse as she unlocks the door that connects the nurses' station to the unit. As the nurse returns to the safety of her station, I quickly run back to my room. I want to get as far away from that tiny locked cell as possible. I decide right then that I have to get out of this place, any way that I can, and the sooner the better.

As the days wear on I feel more and more like a trapped animal. My doctor keeps promising that the unit will protect me from my hallucinations, but that is proving to be a lie time and again. The hopes for safety and security that I had when I first arrived in the unit have changed to feelings of dread and panic. I now have nowhere to run from the spiders, I am locked in a cage, trapped with my demons, and the thought of being trapped in a quiet room again with the spiders is beyond comprehension.

I ask my doctor every day to be released—repeatedly I am told that if I try to leave the unit, he will get an emergency order to have me involuntarily committed; but it doesn't matter, I am already working on a plan for my escape. My fellow partner in incarceration, Kate, also desperately wants off of the unit and it is not long before we are feverishly plotting our breakout together. Over the next couple of days Kate and I take turns watching the traffic going in and out of the door of the locked unit. The escape will be tricky due to the fact that the door is at a 90-degree angle to the nursing station and in plain view of the nursing staff. Undeterred by this seemingly impossible situation, Kate and I forge ahead with the development of our escape plan. After watching the door for a few hours, we notice that when there is a lot of traffic going in and out of the I.C.U. door, it would sometimes stay open a crack. We also notice that when traffic is especially heavy, the visitors coming into the unit instinctively hold the door open for other people as they walk in or out. Since we are in our street clothes, it is hard to tell in a crowd, who are the patients and who are the visitors. Kate and I decide to stake out the door and wait until the traffic becomes very heavy, sooner or later an unsuspecting visitor will unwittingly hold the door open for us and we can simply slip out unnoticed. We catch a break in less than a day. It is right after lunch and there are numerous visitors coming to see inpatients. We cannot believe our good fortune, there is literally a crowd of people forming at the nurses' station window, asking for information about their loved ones. The throng obliterates any view that the nursing staff might have of the locked unit door. In no time, to our great surprise and amazement, a family member who is just arriving, actually holds the door wide open for us. We thank him for the courtesy and quickly slip through the door to freedom.

I keep looking behind us, as we walk through the unlocked unit and out onto the lawn I have admired from afar for so long. As we make our way towards the main building in front of the hospital, Kate, who is twenty years my senior, quickly takes charge of the situation. I am happy to let her dictate where we go next. I trust my special sorority sister and within minutes she leads me past the main building and down the long driveway to the street. Several cars pass us while we walk down the main driveway leading to the hospital, and I wince as each one drives by; sure that a staff member will recognize us and strip us of our new found freedom. To my astonishment, we not only make it down the hill, but out onto the street. Kate doesn't seem to have a care, but I am constantly looking over my shoulder, fully expecting to see a staff member running after us. There is no one in sight.

We are truly free, and we stretch our arms to the sky as we skip down the sidewalk, glowing with a deep feeling of accomplishment. I haven't felt this good in a long time, but reality soon kicks in. As Kate blazes a trail from the hospital to the nearest gas station, I follow. It is a struggle to keep pace with her long, swift strides and I start wondering just what am I going to do out in the middle of a strange town. The area had looked much safer by car, but now it looks quite desolate and a bit dangerous. I ask Kate if she thinks we have made a mistake and she replies with an emphatic "NO". I am in a state of confusion and self-doubt; what am I going to do now? We have no car, no money, and no identification, just the abused casual clothes we are wearing. We look like a couple of street bums out for a stroll.

As we continue our journey, I get the distinct feeling that Kate has done this before. She seems so casual about the entire affair and walks like she knows exactly where she is going. I can't understand why she is not as concerned about our situation as I am. The strain of my predicament is getting to me and after an hour of run–walking down unrecognizable streets and alleyways I inevitably start hallucinating. Gripped with fear, I tell my friend that I want to go back. She tells me in a rather hostile voice, "If you want to go back that is fine, but there is no way I am going back there", and with that she takes off down the street, turns a corner and is gone–just like that.

Now I am all alone in a strange town, and to make matters worse I don't think I can find my way back to the hospital by myself. I start looking for a phone booth when the angry soprano starts up. The angry soprano has to pick now of all times to put on a concert. She calls me "stupid" again and again and screeches the word "bitch" until my head feels like it is going to explode from the decibel level. This puts me into a full–blown panic attack and I know in my gut that the spiders are not far behind. I start crying uncontrollably as I run down the street towards what looks like a pay phone. My fear grows with each passing step and to add to my panic there are surprisingly few cars on the road and the sidewalks seem eerily empty and deserted. I am shaking violently as I pick up the phone and dial information. The operator has to ask me four times to repeat the name of the hospital since my speech is unintelligible through the panic and tears. I dial the hospital collect and when the operator answers, I start ranting hysterically on the phone. The operator at the hospital puts me directly through to my doctor. By now, everyone knows that I have escaped and there is an all out search underway. I tell my doctor that I am alone in the middle of a strange neighborhood and am about to be attacked by the spiders. He tries to calm me down by asking me why I left. I tell him I just had to get outside, that I couldn't take being locked up for so long. He asks me where I am and I tell him between sobs that I have no idea. He asks me to describe what I can see nearby and he quickly ascertains my location. He tells me he will send a cab to pick me up and not to move until it arrives. I promise to stay put and reluctantly hang up the phone; my lifeline gone, I wait for what seems like an eternity for the cab to show up and rescue me.

The cab arrives, and the driver gets out of the car and asks me if I am Tracy Harris. I give him an emphatic "yes" and he helps me into the cab. He treats me as if I am a lost lamb out in the barren wilderness; it is obvious he has done this before. Owning a cab near a mental hospital, he probably picks up "escapees" all of the time. As we get closer to the hospital, I start to question whether I have done the right thing by calling my doctor. I do not have much time to contemplate my decision. Before I know it, we are back at the hospital and the cabby is walking me back to the I.C.U.. The patient cab driver waits with me until a nurse comes to the window to buzz me in. A nurse quickly leads me back into the unit and deposits me in the dining room. She surely is going to scold me for running away, but not a word is said. Later on I find out from one of the patients that while I was gone they had overheard my doctor chewing out the nursing staff for allowing a psychotic and suicidal patient to escape from a locked unit. He had a good point.

I sit down in the dining room, numb and nervous, reflecting on the past two hours. All I can think to do is call home. My father relays to me that during my tiny flight of freedom, my doctor had called them and they had been calling the unit every few minutes frantic for any news about my whereabouts. I instantly feel an intense sense of shame. How could I have put them through even more pain? What kind of person does that to people they love? I beg my dad for forgiveness and try to sound as together as possible, as if anything can make them feel better after this latest kick in the teeth. As the phone call winds down, the spiders start in again and I quickly say my goodbyes to the family and hang up the phone. If only I could have my tape player, even for a few minutes. All I need is my Chopin, just one movement of Chopin and I know I will be all right. I go to my room feeling desperate and foolish.

Shortly, thereafter, a nurse walks up to me and asks me to "accompany her" to the nurses' station. I know exactly what that means and I flatly refuse to go anywhere with her. This particular nurse has a high-pitched voice that is irritatingly squeaky and tends to break a lot. Her voice reminds me of a beginning flutist cracking a high note, unable to coordinate airspeed with embouchure placement. Again she squawks her demand and follows it up with a threat. She states, "You will absolutely follow me to the nurses' station or I will get more members of the staff to help persuade you". I ask her once more why I have to go to the nurses' station and she flatly states that it is "doctor's orders".

I decide not to make matters worse and give in to her demand. I follow her slowly down the hall, into the nurses' station. She walks me to the quiet room and asks me to sit on the bed. I am being punished for being a bad patient. Now they are going to use every tool in their medical arsenal to make me suffer for making them "look bad". I have gotten them in big trouble and they are going to make me pay with the worst sentence available to them, indefinite incarceration in a quiet room. The nurse walks back out of the room and leaves the door open. My mind is racing. Are they going to strap me to the bed? Has she gone for reinforcements? She quickly returns with a second nurse in tow. She hands me a pill and asks me to swallow it. I ask her what it is and she says, "It's just something to calm you down". I don't believe her but I have no choice in the matter. I swallow the pill and she tells me to lie down. I beg the nurses to let me go back to my room. I apologize profusely for causing any trouble and promise I will be good. I am told that the decision is my doctor's and they can't go against his orders. Fortunately they do not put me in restraints. They leave the room and I am left alone, locked in this silent cell of concrete and glass. I cannot breathe in this terrible room, which seems even smaller than before and soon I am gasping for air; claustrophobia is now in charge. I scream for them to let me out and I pace the floor, intermittently pounding on the small glass window on the door, pleading for anyone to "Please let me out". The walls start to close in on me and I am convinced I am suffocating. Soon I am incredibly dizzy. My arms and legs are tingling; they feel like they are being pricked with thousands of sharp pins, over and over again. My breathing is becoming increasingly labored, if only I could get one good, deep breath. My hands start to warp into bizarre looking claws and they soon feel like they have been cemented together. As I pass out, I can hear the faint din of my singing companion. Her aria of "bitch, bitch, bitch" fills my ears and for a few moments I feel less alone in my chamber of death. Then all goes black.

The next thing I know, I feel someone pulling at my arm, trying to get me to stand. I shake my head and try to hear the orders that are being shouted at me. "Tracy, get up and sit on the bed. Come on, you need to get on the bed". I have passed out on the floor next to the bed in a rumpled heap. I don't know how long I have been out, and the nurses look very concerned. I shakily get to my feet with one nurse pulling on each arm and I sit on the bed. My arms and hands are still tingling and I feel lightheaded. My hands don't seem to want to move and all of my limbs feel like lead weights. I tell the nurses that I cannot breathe and one of them runs out of the room and quickly returns with a paper bag. I am told to breathe as regularly as I can into the bag. The nurse puts the bag to my face and with each jagged breath out, the bag expands to its full size and as I breathe in, the bag collapses against my face. I am not suffocating after all; rather I am getting too much oxygen causing me to hyperventilate. After a few minutes of breathing into the paper bag I am starting to feel better. The tingling is starting to subside and I can move my fingers again. After a few minutes, the tingling has abated and my breathing is slow and steady. The nurse instructs me to lie down on the bed and try to relax. I tell her I cannot breathe in this room, especially with the door shut. The diva nurse takes pity on me, and asks me if I would feel better if she left the door open and I answer, "Yes, please". Starting to feel the effects of the heavy sedation, I fall asleep within minutes.

I am awakened by a loud male voice telling me to wake up. I quickly jump off of the hard bed and see a male nurse standing in the doorway. I have never seen this nurse before. He reminds me of the classic overweight opera tenor with his big belly and manicured beard. His low, deep voice and careful diction simply add to the operatic illusion. He tells me that they need the room and that I am once again free to go back into the unit. I think to myself, Free? Is he kidding? A cage is a cage, it doesn't matter the size. *"Stone walls do not a prison make nor iron bars a cage", but they are sure a good facsimile. (*Richard Lovelace, cavalier, poet and ancestor)

I stumble out of the room and follow the nurse to the I.C.U. door and with the turn of a key I am back in the unit, thankful to be out of the suffocating closeness of the quiet room. Within a couple of minutes, I hear a man screaming profanities at the top of his lungs. I look to see who is making the noise and see a man being wheeled into one of the quiet rooms strapped to a gurney. He has come in by ambulance and is extremely agitated. Every nurse in the place has put gloves on and they all squeeze into the quiet room to help move the uncooperative man from the gurney to the bed. It takes quite a while to get him off the gurney and into restraints and the man never stops screaming. The clamor causes quite a stir amongst the patients and we all gather together outside the nurses' station window. None of us say anything; it is a very disturbing sight. A nurse sees us all standing there and opens the window above the station. She tells us there is nothing to see and orders us all back to our appointed cells. As we reluctantly make our way back down the hallway to our rooms, we can still hear the poor man's cries for help. I feel sorry for him, but at the same time I thank God it isn't me.

As I walk back to my room, it suddenly strikes me that I have not seen Kate since being brought back to the unit. Where is she? Has she made it home? I quickly search the small unit for her, but she is nowhere to be found. I ask a nurse in one of the patient's rooms if Kate had been brought back and the nurse states with great disgust that "She has not turned up yet". Even though I am still mad at Kate for leaving me standing in the street alone, I feel a deep sense of loss. Now who am I going to talk to? Kate is the only one who helps me take my mind off of my troubles. It is too much to contemplate and I am still feeling sleepy from the medication, so I go back to my room and fall into bed.

The same male nurse who let me out of the quiet room awakens me a few hours later. I am told to come and eat dinner. As I trudge out into the hallway, my head is buzzing and the steamy, stinky aroma of dinner is making its way down the hall, determined to saturate every room in the unit. As I walk into the dining room, there she is. Kate is back! I cannot believe it. I sit down next to her on the couch and she looks at me guiltily. I ask her how they found her and she told me that they had called the cops on her and had her dragged back to the unit. We commiserate with each other, but neither of us truly regrets our actions. We both agree that we will not try it again and attempt to eat some of our dinner. I am surprisingly hungry from the day's excitement and actually eat most of what is on my tray despite its less than appealing flavor.

The next morning I have to face my doctor for the first time since running away, and needless to say, he is not a happy man. I tell him that I am not sorry for leaving. He had driven me to it by keeping me cooped up for so long. It is his fault, not mine. He tells me in his most authoritative voice, "We will be watching you very closely from now on". He increases my medication and my speech is slightly slurred after that. My mind floats from hour to hour unable to focus on much of anything due to the thick fog of medications that numb my brain. Kate and I compare notes after she has seen her doctor. I am incredulous when Kate relays to me that her doctor blames her for the whole thing. He accused her of being a bad influence on me, and of taking advantage of someone who is "much younger and profoundly sicker" than she is.

I took umbrage with the idea that I was sicker than Kate. After all, aren't we both in the I.C.U.? The notion that Kate suffers from a less severe degree of madness eats at me. It is like comparing a Beethoven symphony to a Mozart symphony. Both are incomparable and both are innately beautiful. Can one honestly make the case that one is somehow more beautiful than the other? Kate and I are both sick, and we both suffer from our very own unique madness. How can one madness be truly worse than another? The implications are disturbing to me. If Kate is really less mad than I, then perhaps levels of madness more severe await me. Can I be afflicted with an even worse form of madness than I already suffer from? I cannot fathom anything worse than this.

The comment Kate's doctor made sticks with me and I begin sizing up the other patients in the unit. I have some distorted need to know that I do not hold first place in the madness rankings. Someone in the unit has to have a mind more off–tuned than my own. It is a terrible reality, but just as our society ranks who is a better person based on what a person looks like on the outside, patients with mental problems often rank people based on what they look like on the inside. People don't like to admit it, but they are relieved when they see other people who are not as attractive or as smart as they are. That means that there is someone else out there who has the dubious honor of being ranked last. Nobody wants to come in last, not even mental patients. It makes no rational sense to worry about an imaginary ranking of mental fitness among us, but I still spend hours sitting in the dining room observing my fellow patients. I make a mental tally of each symptom they display; as sick as I am, someone has to be sicker.

After dinner, I sit in a chair across from the grape juice stained couch, watching a new admission come in. She is a young woman, very quiet, who was admitted right before dinner. She was sent to the hospital from the county mental health facility because they had no beds left. She appears extremely psychotic, talking to the wall and mumbling softly to an imaginary creature that she calls Satan. I start to cheer up; she has to be sicker than me. I am moving up in the rankings. I watch as the nurse gives the new admission some pills to swallow to quell the sounds in her head. The young girl swallows the pills compliantly and she watches as the nurse leaves the room. I can hardly believe what I see next. In plain view of everyone in the room, she sticks her finger down her throat and vomits up all of the pills she has just taken directly onto the floor. She starts shouting about how the pills are poison and that everyone is trying to kill her. I run to get a nurse who impatiently cleans up the vomit and tries to give her the pills again; to our astonishment she vomits the new pills up as well. I feel for the young woman but at the same time I am frightened by just how sick she is and I quickly walk out of the room. I suddenly feel terrible for trying to "rank" my fellow patients. Who am I to judge? I decide that is a job reserved exclusively for the Almighty Himself.

The days in the unit turn into weeks and each day seems like an eternity. I watch day after day as patients are transferred out of the I.C.U. and moved to the freedom of "the other side" while I am left behind. Even Kate finally gets out. She promises to visit me once she gets settled on the other unit, but I don't expect to see her again. Who would want to be reminded of their incarceration in the I.C.U. or of the concentrated suffering that resides behind its locked door?

As the weeks pass I know unequivocally that the medications are not working for me and my hallucinations persist. My desire to be rid of my existence is just as intense as it was the day I was admitted. I decide to confront my doctor one morning with the fact that I am not getting better and perhaps it is due to the fact that the medication I am taking is not the right medication for me. I am dumbfounded by his reaction. He is defensive and evasive telling me that I do not know what is best for me and I just have to "trust" that it is all going to be o.k. I tell him I am tired of trusting and tired of waiting. If I have to suffer like this, I want to do it in the comfort of my own bed and be able to use my own bathroom whenever I choose.

My doctor is so cold and unfeeling that I believe he does not hear my anguished requests for relief. I can only assume that his unimpassioned responses are due to his own inner confusion as to the method of treatment that can rid me of my terrible delusions. As I would find out later, if this doctor had made the proper diagnosis and given me the appropriate medications, he would not have needed to respond as though he were speaking to someone with a contagion that alchemists would have blamed on the punishments dealt out by their God. Ironically, my physician shared some of society's most common misconceptions about the mentally ill. He treated me as if I were incapable of making any type of rational observations about myself, or my medical care. He, like so many others treated the mentally ill as if their malady had somehow lowered their intelligence quotient. It did not take a genius to see that I still looked just as frail, exhausted, hopeless and lost as I did the day of my admission to this supposedly healing institution, and because of that fact, I wanted answers. More importantly I wanted accountability. Why does my physician treat me like an uneducated idiot whenever I want to discuss my medication regimen or my dosages? Admittedly, I am actively suicidal and at times I suffer from a form of psychosis, but that does not preclude me from having a mind that is capable of rational thought and logical analysis when the situation calls for it. After days of stonewalling from my doctor about different treatment options, I resolve to get out of this "heavenly" asylum.

I call my parents after my doctor and I have words for the third day in a row. The fact that he is so unwilling to even consider trying other medications, or other dosages of the medications I am already taking, is mind–boggling to me. I tell my family that I want to get the hell out of this place. Fortunately for me, my parents have already noticed the inelastic views of my doctor and the fact that I am simply not getting any better. They had already launched their own intensive search for a psychopharmacologist who could help me. Over the next couple of days, my family and I plan my "liberation" from the place that at once held such promise in my mind, but now has me trapped in a cycle of mistreatment and persistent illness.

The key to my escape plan is to get outside. I have to convince my doctor that he can trust me enough to let me out for lunch. I have not been let outside since I had escaped from the unit, so the odds of him allowing me to feel the sun's warmth on my face are rather slim, so my parents ask my doctor if I can have a picnic lunch with them at the hospital. After some persistence on my father's part, my doctor grudgingly agrees to let me out for lunch. On the morning of my liberation, I meet with my unsuspecting doctor who states that I will not be allowed to eat lunch out on the front lawn of the hospital, unless I compose and sign a "disclaimer" that states in my own words that I promise not to try and escape again. So I dutifully write down my promise to him, stating that I will not attempt to escape again. I cannot believe that a few words on a piece of paper mean the difference between freedom or incarceration and I am baffled as to how my live words seem to mean nothing to my doctor, but a few choice words on a piece of paper somehow magically change his entire attitude towards me and my mental health.

Once I finish writing my hollow promises, I carefully fold the note into a small square and walk it up to the nurses' station. With confidence, I hand it to the nurse and ask her to please give it to my doctor as soon as possible. My doctor keeps his promise and after reading the note, tells me that I will be allowed to go outside and have lunch with my family. I run to the unit phone and in hushed tones tell my father that our escape plans are on schedule. My father excitedly tells me that after tireless research they have found the right doctor for me, a highly respected psychopharmacologist in Los Angeles and have already scheduled an appointment for me to meet with him. When I hang up the phone I feel an emotion I thought I had all but abandoned, HOPE.

I spend the rest of the morning preparing for my get away by inconspicuously gathering my things. They can have the items, including my hairdryer, that they have been "holding for me" for my own "protection"; such is the price of freedom.

When my parents arrive, it is hard to quell the nervous excitement I am feeling at the prospect of leaving this place forever. My escape is surprisingly simple. I walk to the locked door of the unit with my parents in tow and ask for the nurse diva to open the door. She reaches under the counter and presses a button and the door pops open. It couldn't be simpler. I practically run through the door and my parents and I make a hasty retreat to our car that is stationed at the ready out in the parking lot. As I approach our car, I can see my brother sitting in the front seat and he has the engine running. I feel like I have just held up a bank as my dad leaps into the front seat and my mother and I pile into the back seat and with the slam of a couple of car doors and a decidedly firm foot on the accelerator, we quietly speed away—out of the doctor's sight, out of the Vistas' sight, out of the sight of the diva nurse and once more head into the real world. I am FREE. As we drive away, I do not look back for fear of turning into a pillar of salt. I look forward to a life that can begin once again. I would soon be seeing a physician who would put an end to my mind's crazy cadenza.

6

Recovering My Mind's Inner Harmony

Quieting The Discord Within

I am actually leaving the hospital. As we drive away, those words begin to sink deep into my consciousness. I have gained my freedom from the conditions I so hated in the Vistas of Heaven, but as we drive farther away from that institution, I realize I still have an unwanted guest in my family's car. The angry soprano is still with me. Even as I look towards the future with the hope of proper medication and the right doctor, the imperious voice in my head is still telling me, "You still can't do anything right, you stupid bitch. What makes you think you can escape me as easily as you escaped that mental institution? You are never going to find a cure and I will make sure I am there when you try to play your music once again. Check the door, is it locked? All you need to do is pull the latch up and you can open the door, it's just that easy. Jump out now, you've got nothing left to save anyway." I try humming my favorite piano concerto by Chopin. I need to concentrate on those beautiful notes. I don't want to open the door. My family is here. Safety is here. And yet I still hear that voice. I move closer to my mother who is in the back seat with me and without any words spoken, she quickly puts her arms around my shoulders, pulling me towards her in a gesture of comfort; a gesture I have grown up with. My mother understands; as she always has. The diva did not understand. My unholy doctor at the Vista did not understand. But thank God my mother is here at last and she understands.

The horrors of the Vistas of Heaven still ring within my head with the distorted overtones of a cracked bell. I look forward to seeing my bed at home once again and the warmth and security that my family affords, but I come to my home bearing the same wounds for which I had sought help when I entered The Vistas. I have come home from the war, still not healed and desperately in need of the salve of the doctor's magic potion. I know that I will have love during these desperate hours. I hope that I will also have a doctor with the knowledge to make my mind whole again. As the car slows down and pulls into our driveway, some of my first optimism upon leaving the hospital has already become dull and mixed with the distorted messages that are jabbing at the insides of my brain. My mother, still holding me close to her, walks me slowly to my bedroom and for a brief moment I fear that I have just reentered the same places in my mind that I had tried to escape through death.

Of course, there are repercussions. My doctor is on the phone with my father as soon as we arrived home asking about my whereabouts, fortunately for me, my father convinces him to transfer my care to the new physician they had found in Los Angeles. I think my doctor is more than happy to be rid of me. I was a "problem patient" and had made more than a few problems for him while I was in the unit.

(My personal effects bag arrived a couple of days later from the hospital and unbelievably, sitting next to my hairdryer, lay the razor blade they had taken from me when I was first admitted. Fortunately for me, I no longer needed it.)

I sit for a long time on the side of my bed with my mother sitting next to me and I sob quietly as she rocks my body back and forth in a gesture of love that I need to bring my soul back to my home and my family. "It's going to be alright", she says, over and over, as if she understands how difficult it is for me to believe. I desperately want to, but the voice in my head keeps intruding, assuring me that it will not be all right. My mother suggests that I lie down and rest, while she makes my favorite soup. She walks slowly out of the room, looking back as though she does not want to lose contact with me during these fragile moments. I look slowly around my bedroom and it seems somehow changed. I look at the small clock near my bed that has shared the horrible moments of my mind's distorted reality and I think just briefly of the scratching of the Tarantella and the ugliness of the black spiders. I try to focus my mind's thoughts on happier moments. I no longer need to get permission from the diva nurse to urinate. I can walk into the kitchen, free to select real food from my own refrigerator and use a fork and real knife without someone taking it from my hands. I continue to remind myself that the world that I want to live in–this reality that I want to make my own–is a free world inhabited by people with free souls. I desperately want to join them again and share their life. Making their life and their reality, my reality. I want my soul and my life and myself back.

I slowly look around the room for my flute. It is still in its case, untouched. I tentatively walk the few feet to where it lies and gently pick it up. I take it to my bed and sit down with it on my lap. For many moments I stare at the case, its clasps still closed, and then I pick it up as though a baby and hold it next to my bosom. I hear the faint sounds of my last concert; as though I were playing it while watching myself from the back of the concert hall. The music stirs feelings in me that I have not felt for what seems like a lifetime. I put the case back down on my lap and slowly open it until I can see the flute nestled within its protective home. I touch it ever so gently with the tips of my fingers and without lifting it from its case I begin again to softly cry. Just the thought of placing the flute to my lips is a joy I have almost completely forgotten. But, as with anticipating a lover's kiss, I just continue to stroke the flute in its case and rock gently back and forth but do not bring it to my lips, allowing the remembrance of performances and the sounds that I love, to replace the kiss of the lover no longer with me. I slowly lie back on my bed and for the first time since I had entered the Vistas of Heaven, I sleep the peaceful sleep of purification.

I awake to the familiar sounds of birds that occupy the trees near my bedroom and feel the bright warming fingers of sunlight crossing my body. I stretch the long slow stretch of the warrior, having finished one battle, just to begin another. I have slept all night–dreamlessly, giving me the strength I need to begin what I hope is the start of the final fight. I remind myself that today is the day I will meet that special doctor my parents have found for me. My parent's have given me great hope and I feel that somehow my answer will come at last through the miracles of this new doctor's alchemy.

After finishing a breakfast that the inmates of the Vistas of Heaven could only dream about, I return to my room to prepare for the long drive to Los Angeles where my new doctor's office is located. I prepare as carefully as I did for my last performance when I was planning my death. But in this case, I am planning the renewal of my life and the sanctification of my ideas, my soul and my will. Once fully dressed, I glance quickly at myself in the mirror, and ask for brief approvals from my mother, my sister and my sister–in–law, who have now crowded into my room. They all nod and make the appropriate compliments to make me feel very wanted, appreciated and loved. My mother is first. She straightens a bit of my clothing and states her approval quietly. My sister smiles and silently gives me a thumbs up and my sister–in–law, after a long look nods her approval and gives me a quick hug.

My parents had decided to accompany me on this first visit to this new doctor. A doctor who understood the pharmacology of the brain as well as its dynamics and did not rely solely on analysis techniques to try to pull from my poor, tired, consciousness, the answers that those other healers did not have. After speaking to several experts on the east coast and inquiring as to the availability of the proper medical help on the west coast, they were led to a psychopharmacologist who I will call Dr. G.. His offices are located near the Pacific Ocean in West Los Angeles.

My first visit with Dr. G. is in itself a great revelation in that I have found someone who treats my disease as a real physical infirmity, rather than presenting a need for hours of psychotherapy or asking how I feel about the tough, yellow skin of an over–ripe banana.

That day, Dr. G. presented real solutions based on science and a deep understanding of the brain and psychopharmacologic expertise that included manipulation of the complex chemistry required to make my mind whole once again. This first meeting with Dr. G. was a revelation to me in many ways; not only was he well versed in the tools of his science, but he relied on fighting my disease through modifications of my brain chemistry and changes in my neurohormonal conditions, and not solely on psychotherapy. Dr. G. immediately prescribed several possible drug therapies, which would lessen my inner turmoil, diminish my delusions and allow me to directly do battle with the suffocating depression, bizarre mania and the angry voice within my head. Dr. G. was professional in every way and yet had a gentleness that reflected a real concern for the human condition and for those who are mentally ill. This was the first doctor I had met who did not either directly or indirectly blame me for my illness, but rather looked to the physiological and biological aspects of my special brain and how he could deal with its information processing through therapeutic chemical treatment. He indicated to me at this and the next few visits that he would use a range of drug therapies depending on my response and the effects that they might have on my ability to lead my life in a more normal fashion. Unlike the other doctors I had seen, he did not have one favorite drug therapy, because as he stated, every person is somewhat different in terms of their body responses and their individual uptake of the drugs they are given. It was after many in depth visits that Dr. G. diagnosed my condition as Schizoaffective Disorder. As he said those words to me, I felt the cold reality that only a serious diagnosis can bring. Even though I had known before I came to this doctor that I was seriously ill, it was my own inner prejudices against this type of mental illness that gave to me this terrifying response. His words could just as well have been, "You have cancer of the brain and only a short time to live". I tried to compose myself as quickly as possible and asked, with my voice shaking, "Can I ever live a normal life again?" Dr. G. leaned closer to me and looked directly into my eyes, with that look that I would soon become used to seeing and told me the first words of encouragement that I had been given by a doctor relative to this mental condition, "You have a serious illness, I won't deny you that and it's quite rare to see patients like you still moving about and functioning at such a high level. Yes, Tracy there is hope. There is medication now that can help you lead a more normal life and there are even more exciting medications being tested this very moment. I promise you, that together with the aid of these medications, we will overcome the devastation to your mind." As Dr. G. said these words, I felt the beginnings of new life stirring within those dark corners of my fatigued mind. Dr. G. was not only a capable doctor, he was also a warm gentle man with piercing eyes that seemed to look deep into my troubled mind to search for answers and to diagnose the very nature of the illness that existed there while quietly assuring me that I will prevail. I felt the strength of his support through his gestures and the almost noble responses to the difficult mix of questions that crowded my mind and for which I had no answers. I was convinced by the third visit that with Dr. G.'s help and guidance, together with my family's love and support, I could return to the music that I loved and begin to shape my broken career once again. I was ready to do battle with the angry soprano and with the help of my new physician that battle would be fought with new tools and in a new arena, which favored my victory and her defeat.

It was time for me to reacquaint myself with my flute. The reclaiming of my music was a long, slow procedure. I remember entering my studio and picking up my flute in its case time and again, only to put it back down and leave the house to walk amongst the trees and watch my horse in the distance. My mother would softly nudge me to play by asking in her own special way how it was going and did my flute sound any better? I knew what she was asking, but I was not prepared to tell her that I still had not played my flute.

But then it happened. I woke up one morning and looked briefly outside to see if it was cloudy or sunny and calmly walked over to where my flute was lying in its case, assembled the parts and began to play The Hungarian Fantasy by Doppler. I was playing my flute; I was actually playing once more. My heart leapt into my mouth and I almost dropped my flute out of sheer surprise, but I continued to play. I felt that my fingers could not reach some of the places they used to reach so easily, they felt clumsy and I gasped for air in the wrong places; but I was playing the flute again. I almost wanted to stop and scream as loud as I could until the hills could hear the echo: "I can play!" I wanted to run outside the house and tell my family wherever they were and tell the animals that I love and tell the very pasture grass that's under my feet I can play the flute once more, I can make the music I love. I know I am not cured, but now I can begin to do what has always been in my soul, speaking to others through my music. Of course my flute playing that day was less than perfect; my breath support was gone, my embouchure was not quite right, my fingers would not always follow my commands, but I was playing music again and some of the importance of my life had returned. Yes, I still could hear some voices. Yes, the medication did not shine light on all of those dark places that had overtaken my mind, but after the emptiness of the quiet room of The Vistas and the depths that my depression had reached, I was a flutist once again. I sat outside my house, in the deep grass, holding my flute and dreaming those early dreams once again of filling my life with emotion through the sounds of my music and transmitting that joy to an audience that would be enraptured by the sounds that I made. I lay back in the deep grass and made plans for my return to the concert hall. I lay there with my eyes shut feeling the sun through my closed eyelids with the cold metal of the flute in my hands, while the warm westerly breeze washes across my face and reminds me how beautiful life can be. I stay that way, almost motionless, absorbing the fullness of life until the warm breezes of midday turn to the coolness of another evening. Happier than I had been since this terrible illness began, I stood up and reentered my house to begin the rest of my career.

I sat at dinner that night talking to my parents, but thinking only of my music. I cannot tell you what the food was that my parents served that night or if I even ate, all I knew and all I could think of and all I could surround myself with was the work of music that I had lost to a thousand cuts and degradations of my reality.

I slept that night, again in solitude, without the voices or the nightmare realities that had been my life through this illness. The medication seemed to be working its miracle. I was comfortable with the thought that I would be performing once again. What I did not know is that it would take other combinations of medications and other small skirmishes to fully control the angry soprano and the other delusions that I lived with in my changing reality. But for now, I felt that I was on the path which led to a rich useful life in which death became the shadow, transparent and weak as one sees it who is full of life.

The next morning I awoke quickly, jumped out of bed as though it was Christmas morning and took a brisk walk and a shower to prepare myself for a rigorous day of flute practice. It was almost as though I needed the traditional exercises of the monk or the knight before I went into battle. This day's confrontation with my flute and my reality brought me back to where I needed to be. I still could not play my flute well. The sounds of my music would not enrapture a captive audience and I could not run past a quarter of a mile. But with my delusions fading I could white wash the fence that bounded my reality and see the possibility of new accomplishments. I was ready to joust with the angry soprano.

I sat for a moment contemplating the many steps that would take me from the shakiness of my hands and the lack of breath support to the full performance capability that I would need to play again in front of a live audience. For a moment I felt a sense of discouragement, but the angry voice that had kept me company for so long was weaker on this morning and I thanked God for the medication and the doctor I had found to help me recover the abilities I once had. I sat there with the flute in my hands and said over and over quietly to myself, "I will win this battle. I will play my music again. I will regain my mind." Then, I brought the head joint to my lips and attempted to play a second octave A. As the sounds came forth, they seemed to retain the fatigue that my mind felt. They had lost their clarity and had the fuzzy character of soldiers too long in battle asked to plan an attack for which they were not ready. I tried supporting the sound a bit more and noticed that with even more air support my tone was thin and lacked body, gone was the powerful sonorous tones I had spent years and countless hours perfecting. No, I clearly was not ready. The long separation from my flute due to the requirements of the Vistas of Heaven had done its job on more than my mind; it had affected my music and my hands and my body. Just as my brain still felt unfocused and uncentered, so too did my flute's tone; a reflection of the damage my mental illness had caused to not only my brain but to the character of my body. My instrument was not at fault, but my body as an instrument had failed me. The reality of that moment would normally have sent me into a deep depression, but with the aid of my new medication I took my physical condition as a challenge to be met through work and dedication. I silently recited an oath to myself to never let the instrument that was my body fall into disrepair to the extent that it would affect my ability to play my flute and make the music that I was born to generate. I set about the exercises I knew I must complete to give me the strength that my instrument required. I began physical exercises; I ran, I increased the volume of my breathing. I would run upstairs just for the joy of feeling my heart pound and the depth of the air I could consume in my lungs. I was truly preparing for a battle and I knew that my body must catch up with my brain for my talent to show once more.

My sound was the most important component of my musical art. My flute's tone gave me the ability to sing in such a way that the listener could feel what I was feeling as I played and be touched as I was touched by the turn of a phrase or the diminuendo of a silvery high G. My tone was my vehicle of expression, the special way I spoke to others through my music. The importance of resonance and projection combined with a clarity and roundness of tone cannot be discounted as perhaps the most important aspect of the flute and as I stood alone in the center of my studio, playing one weak scale after another until the muscles in my face ached and my lips burned, I realized how much of my music had been stolen by my illness.

Although my physical workouts were helping me to feel stronger and were giving me the strength I needed for the challenges of a full concert, I still had problems with those parts of my body which could only be exercised properly through the use of my flute. After a long jog outside, I would go back to my studio and pick up my flute as a continuation of my exercises, but, after barely twenty minutes of long tones and rudimentary scales, my lips began to shake from exhaustion and although I felt strength in the rest of my body, I was forced to stop and put my flute down. I wept tears of deep frustration as I cleaned my instrument. It had not lost its vitality. It did not have voices forcing it to change its mechanism of my art. It was ready as ever to join with me and create the beautiful music that was my life before this mental illness. My mind knew on an intellectual level, all of the mechanics that were needed to produce a good sound. I knew the proper placement of my embouchure, I knew the proper alignment of the head joint on my chin, yet I was unable to produce a tone even close to the quality I had possessed before I became so ill. Besides the apparent atrophy of the muscles in my lips, the new medications prescribed by my doctor had their own devastating effects. Although they were helping my mind, they were literally changing the dynamics of my body.

Along with these many differing medications came many kinds of side effects. Some were benign in their result, and others were so significant that they forced me to drop the medication immediately. One such medication gave me a buzzing in my head that was more extreme than anything I had experienced from the angry soprano. It had caused a tinnitus so powerful that I literally could not think or function. After one call to my doctor, that medication was removed and another put in its place. Another combination produced a type of delusion that I had never experienced. These delusions had much of the same qualities of the nightmarish images I had experienced before, but they had the lack of reality which transparency can give to what would otherwise seem real. I saw people standing near me but I knew that they did not exist except in my mind because they were almost completely transparent. I saw bugs and spiders that would normally put fear into my heart except for the fact that they were almost clear and devoid of color. Needless to say, I changed drugs once again. Another interesting drug variation submerged me into a world of uncontrollable laughter. Everything—literally everything—was funny. And even though I was laughing on the outside, inside I was considering another variation in my medication. Fortunately, this particular effect did not last for more than a few days. I developed a tremor in both hands and little annoying ticks in my fingers. I developed a balance problem which was serious enough that I had to stop driving and could only go out of the house with a family member or with the aid of a taxi. I had difficulty waking up, and I had difficulty going to sleep. My time was filled with crying spells for no apparent reason and my hearing became so sensitive that sounds were magnified to the point of physical pain. And if they were too loud I would hear echoes of the sounds within my head. For a time, food lost its flavor and became faintly reminiscent of the over-cooked, over-boiled cuisine that was served to me as a guest of the Vistas of Heaven. My skin became so sensitive that even the lightest touch felt as though I had been dealt a heavy blow. All of my medications, although they helped greatly to decrease my delusions, depression and manic states, brought with them a heavy price; the disruption of my normal senses. Through various changes in my medications Dr. G.

managed to free me of most of the side effects except for a very dry mouth and a certain loss of my short-term memory. Because my mouth was made very dry it became almost impossible to produce the type of tone that I felt was so important. I would drink large quantities of water whenever I practiced in a vain attempt to keep my lips and throat moist. I asked my doctor if there were alternative drug therapies to the ones I was currently taking. I explained that it was affecting my music. He immediately understood the depth of my problem and suggested new medications once more to help me through this difficult period of adjustment. He realized that my music was more than therapy to me; my music, despite all of the horrific hallucinations was not only my life, it was my salvation. These first few months at home with this new drug therapy were filled with my struggles to reconnect with my flute and still fight the continuing voices, depression and hallucinations that had yet to be controlled by the medicine.

It had been about six months since I first met Doctor G. and had begun our search for the best drug therapy for me. All this while I was continuing to improve my physical condition, my mental condition, and my music. One day while in my studio, I noticed, almost as an aside, a distinct change in the character of that horrid voice that had tormented me for so many dark years. I remember, as though it were an epiphany, this hint of a change in the balance of power between myself and that strange voice within me. Somehow my mind seemed less connected to that voice and I could control my attention to the point of ignoring the Soprano's angry words..

I was in my studio playing a Paganini Caprice at a painfully slow tempo in a concerted attempt to regain my technique, as the voice began its epithets, telling me to quit, telling me I could not play this instrument I loved, telling me that it controlled my soul and it was useless to fight. But this time the words of that horrid voice did not bother me. Even though her epithets were meant to hurt me, I felt as though they were being said to someone else and I was able to ignore them for the first time in years of mental anguish. I did not run this time to try and escape that voice. I did not cry. I did not seek the comfort of someone else's arms; I calmly picked up my instrument and simply began to practice the Paganini Caprices again. I realized at that moment that with the help of medication, although my delusions and depression had not disappeared, I had gained an edge over the angry soprano in the continuing battle to regain my life.

As I celebrated silently, once again an almost imperceptible sound joined that of my own thoughts. For a moment I stopped the steady stream of silent accolades. She had returned to do battle once again, it was the angry soprano who had somehow lifted herself from the battlefield and stood fully before me in the arraignments I knew so well. But the wounds of battle were beginning to show. There was an almost indiscernible difference in the ferocity of her voice. I stood very still, but this time my response was different. I was able to listen to this raging voice inside me with a cool detachment I had not thought possible. I knew deep inside my soul that she could never harm me in the same way again. I realized that there would still be other battles to fight. But I knew that I had given her a mortal wound and she could never harm me in the same way again.

As I struggled through the caprice trying to double–tongue the sixteenth notes on the score in front of me, I still felt the elation of this day in which I had met my enemy and remained standing. Even though my tongue felt like it was anesthetized, sluggishly flopping against the roof of my mouth in a vain attempt to grant the notes on the page their proper articulation, I could not overcome the feeling of joy, happiness and triumph on this day.

There in the middle of my studio for the first time, I felt a tiny spark of control over my illness. Emboldened by the voice's seeming loss of dominion over my will, I picked up my flute and began the Paganini once more, carefully playing each note as loudly as I could despite the angry Soprano's protestations. I played on for another twenty minutes while she tried in vain to obliterate the tones of my flute with her own distorted voice until I could sense a retreat from the battlefield. I had won. I had won. I had won!

With each medication adjustment my mental armor increased. I could feel those clouded rooms in my mind, which this illness attempted to control, slowly clearing. The angry soprano began to recede into the shadows away from the center stage of my mind and the spiders and other delusions diminished in intensity along with the bouts of deep depression and manic chaos.

A few more months passed and as my practice sessions became less affected by my mental illness I began to feel stronger and more in control. I asked my sister to play her harp with me to see if I could handle the stress of performing with someone else again. To my surprise and shock she said firmly, "I don't think I want to play the harp with you any more, I'm not sure I know you." I stood there unbelieving—was this the sister that had always been my closest friend? Was this the sister who would cry on my shoulder when she was hurt? I did not know what to say at first. And then I spoke softly to her, watching as the tears flowed down her cheeks. "I know that you have been here to watch me as I struggle with my illness, but I always felt that you understood the anguish that I felt inside me, and you were always there to help when I needed you." Wendy looked back at me, her eyes flashing with anger: "Can you understand", she said, "that I always have felt that I was competing with your voices and with your visions." She continued, sobbing as she spoke, "Sometimes, Tracy, you would be better and I would feel happy and hopeful that life would return to the way it used to be, but then your illness would grip you once again. As inevitably as the seasons turn, you would slip into sudden moments of terrible sadness, and I felt as if our hands could never quite meet even though I reached for you with all my strength. In spite of all that I tried to do, you would slip even farther down into the depths of your depression." "But don't you know," I answered, "that I'm getting better now? Can't you sense, as I do, that the voice in my head is not turning me from you any more? Can't we…"

Just then Wendy interrupted by putting her hands against my arm to quiet my voice; "I know that times were better before your illness. I remember when we used to make plans to get up and sneak into the living room to see all of the presents we would get for Christmas. I remember when we used to stay up late and watch movies and make fun of the shows and laugh. We would throw stuffed animals around the room and jump on our beds. We would ride horses together and explore the hills around our house. You protected me when I was made fun of in school, you saved my life when I almost drowned in the pool at our baby sitter's, and we built tents over our beds and played games together. You stayed up with me when I had bad dreams and you never got mad when I complained or when we talked. We made funny recordings and always talked about the future and what we would be doing. I always looked up to you and wanted to do what you did. We roamed dad's office halls and roller-skated and shopped together. I remember you did not have panic or depression or hallucinations."

"I understand", I said quietly, "but that's when we were young. I want to have our lives together again. I want to make music with you, and I want you to love me as I love you. I am still that same sister that was your partner. I am the same sister that helped you when you were sad, and I can still be the person you once knew." Wendy took my hand tighter in hers. "I do love you, but somehow it's as though you've been away in a foreign land which has changed you, and has changed you into someone who I only partially know. When you first became ill, I remember sitting up with you on long summer nights because you were afraid to go to sleep. I was the first to go to the hospital with you and help you check in when you could no longer help yourself to stay alive. I always took clothes and things to you in the hospital and had to cope with seeing you and not being able to even talk to you because you did not hear me, and in some cases did not recognize me because you were on so much medication." At this point Wendy was sobbing openly. I put my arms around her to comfort her, but this time it did not seem to help. Wendy continued between sobs, "I cried a lot, and I was sad that the illness had taken away my sister, as I knew her. But you were still my sister and I loved you no matter what happened. I tried to understand what you were going through, and was frustrated that I could not make you understand how I felt. That I was hurting too. I know that you are getting better and I am happy for you, but I cannot feel the same sense of recovery. I have had to keep my thoughts hidden for so long because you were going through such horrible moments. I simply drew back from our relationship. I think I was afraid of you. Afraid of your illness. Afraid that it would take you away. Afraid that you would yell at me. Afraid that I would make you worse in some way. You would tell me about the horrible things you were seeing and hearing, and I was scared too, and frustrated that I could not make it go away and that I could never seem to say the right things to comfort you." Wendy stops at that moment and grips both my hands even tighter. And this time, when she looks at me, her eyes have the sweet softness of the love we felt for each other when we were young.

After a deep sigh, Wendy quietly continues, "Despite all of that, I still look up to you. I still love you dearly. I am learning to open up to you again and trust that you are ok. We can be close again. I have always believed that you are a very strong person and I have always been inspired by your ability to overcome such incredible obstacles." At that moment she pulls herself closely to my face and embracing me we both sit there crying as two sisters reunited after a long separation.

After many minutes, I clasp both her hands in mine and I ask her quietly to forgive me. "I am so sorry" she says, "I am so sorry that you have had to live with this terrible illness."

"Of course I forgive you. It has been horrible for you and you do not need my forgiveness—you need my love, and I pray that I have enough strength to give you back all the love we have shared." At that moment Wendy straightens her back and looks to the ceiling as though it could give her the answers to her thoughts. She looks again into my eyes and the words flow from her mouth as though trapped within a levy that has been broken and finally flows freely. "Your illness to me has been like a fast and sickening ride on a roller coaster. I have felt as though I have been in a mad house filled with twisted figures, mirrors and surprises around every turn while I try to keep my balance through a tunnel that constantly turns, keeping me from ever standing upright and keeping me from seeing the world the way it should look. But finally, after this frightening journey of nightmarish horrors, I have come out the other side of that mad house; no, we have come out on the other side together, to find that the daylight and the brightness of life still exists."

As the words spill forth they grow in intensity and fill the room with emotions which have been kept hidden for too long. Wendy continues, "I look back on those early days of your mental illness and remember the frustration that I felt and the helplessness to fight an illness that I did not understand. I remember times when I would walk out to our barn and throw buckets against the walls because I was frustrated and angry. 'How could my sister betray me like that? How could YOU betray me like that? Why did we fight so much? Why did we yell at each other so much?' I was younger than you and I couldn't fully understand what you were going through. I watched as our family desperately tried to help you and I did not know what to do. More and more, I retreated into my own world. I remember finally picking up a book on anxiety disorders and learning about the illness that I thought was affecting you. I could never fully understand what you were going through. Now at last we can talk about it together, and it does not seem as frightening or as frustrating. I no longer fear your illness. I understand. I love you."

It will be many years, if ever, that I will forget that touching conversation with my sister. But she was not the only one affected by my mental illness. All of my family was changed in one way or another by having to live with my madness. I can never erase the memory of sitting on the floor at the foot of my bed while my mother cleaned the numerous cuts on my arms with a cool damp towel. Cuts that I had inflicted on myself with a razor blade while in the throws of a desperate state; an image that has burned itself into my memory and lurks in the black backstage of my mind. I can still see my mother choking back the tears of sorrow that she felt for me. I had never seen that kind of pain in her eyes; the kind of pain that is born out of a mother's feeling of desperate helplessness to ease her daughter's suffering. My mother desperately wanted me to be free of this mental illness that was clutching at the center of my life. She would try to give me hope for the future and a realization that my life was worth something. As devastating as a brain disorder is to the person who suffers from it, I believe that having to live with someone who is mentally ill is equally as difficult and painful as the illness itself. It is almost impossible to express fully just how self-absorbed one can become in the worst days of this illness. When I was in the throws of a deep depression or in the intoxicating blindness of mania, or the warped world of psychosis it was like sitting in the very center of an extremely black narrow tunnel. Noise cannot penetrate through those tunnel walls and the tunnel is so long that I can't detect even a glow of light from either end. In this tunnel it is so dark and isolating that I can't even see my hands in front of me, or feel the presence of others. For the longest time it never occurred to me when I engaged in the act of self-mutilation, or was actively suicidal, that anyone else besides me felt the relentless painful presence of this illness. It took so much energy to fight this disorder that at times it was all I could do to just stay alive.

For years I actually thought that I was hiding my problems from those who loved me the most. I have to struggle every day to keep my perspective, to try and remember that I am not alone in the darkness backstage. I have to constantly remind myself that my actions affect everyone around me. The unpredictability of my moods alone is more than enough to tax anyone let alone the people that care about me the most.

It is my hope that my family's perspective will help others who have had to endure the agony of watching someone they love slowly disintegrate in front of them. Unconditional love is a gift with which I have been blessed. No matter how bad things have gotten my family has stuck by me. Frankly, there were times I was astonished that they didn't pitch me out on the streets. Unconditional love defines an individual in so many glorious ways and my family's love for me was like a wool–warm comforter on a frosty winter night and as lovely and reliable as the sunrise.

Wendy and I had other quiet conversations after this first conversation upon my return home, but none so moving or jarring to my psyche. After all was said, Wendy agreed in spite of her protestations to play the harp with me in recital, and help me to further my dream of making beautiful music.

My sister Wendy and I would spend hours together playing everything from Rossini to Debussy and it seemed the more my playing improved the less mental territory my illness controlled. I was regaining my mind and it felt wonderful. My music was once again my ally rather than an unwilling participant in the disorganization of my mind.

My physical exercise combined with the weakening of my delusions finally gave me the confidence to play a solo recital. I played solo after my first full year of medical therapy. I am still accompanied by the now hushed voice of the angry soprano and I still cannot ignore her. Despite the delusions, I finish my first solo recital and feel once again the warmth and acceptance of audience response at the end of my performance. The medications are allowing me to take one step back from the delusions and see them for what they are; my brain's chemistry gone awry. More local recitals follow and with each succeeding performance I feel stronger—better able to coexist with my disorder, thanks to the insight of my doctor and my medication.

After another year of playing as a soloist, I now feel ready to work with a larger group of instruments as a bridge toward playing with a full symphony once again. I choose a quintet. I select a local hall where I have played before and contact the musicians I will need to play with me. The day of the concert comes quickly and I feel a bit unprepared. I still have some nagging doubts about the strength of that voice that accompanies me silently in concert. Although she is weakened by our battles, she still causes me some concern. Before I know it I am on stage for this important concert and all five of us are checking our intonation one last time.

As the quintet concert beings, I listen intently as the theme to the woodwind quintet by Josef Haydn is gently carried aloft by the unique singing voice of the oboe and then, the message completed, the theme is taken over by the darker tone of the bassoon. Each note of the ensemble adds to the passion of the music. The bassoon embraces this delicate tune like an old companion, enriching it with its low, deep pitches, thus creating a whole new emotion and texture for the melody. I realize at that moment that I am doing more than playing this quintet this evening and it matters little to my life whether this quintet is by Haydn or by Tchaikovsky or by any of the other great musicians—this quintet is my musical experience—this quintet is bringing me back into the world that I have left for so long—this music is allowing me to speak once more in the language I know best, to other human souls around me and to say to them clearly, "Life is wonderful and I want to share its experience with you—and I'm doing it in the best way I can, which is through my music." The music, as it plays out, reflects much of the wide range of emotion that my own life has included in its special music of madness—even though I am one of the players, this music acts upon me and my feelings, in a way that only music can and brings back to me the original sensitivity of my soul, unfettered by the demons of my mind. For me, in the life that I have led so far, music is the language that can be accepted most easily by my mind. It soothes my hurts, it helps explain my nature to others and its forms a bridge across those dark parts of my mind that have been isolated by my illness. It is the very nature of music that can substitute for my words or my ideas, when they are too complicated or too distorted or too filled with the complexities of mental distortion, to allow me to describe my feelings in their purest sense. Music is the vocabulary that allows me to reconnect with the rest of humankind in order to exchange my human feelings with those that share the sameness of our human condition. So I play my flute. I play it as part of this quintet tonight. But through all of this, I am finding my place in life and my true connection with the rest of the world. I know in my heart that a simple passage played by inspired musicians, brings to our ears a set of instrumental voices that have a far greater range of prosody and human feeling than that which can be attained by the same number of human voices. On this night, I listen intently to the rest of the quintet as they play this beautiful work and realize that my voice, through my instrument, gives me my place in the human condition through the playing of my music. This quintet, as in any quintet of inspired musicians, can bring together the texture and color of life itself through the simple and pure medium of music.

I realize as these sounds are produced that I am helping to create a context of emotion and love which produces in my audience more powerful responses to the human feelings we all have than any unlimited set of words could generate. I know now that it is only through my music that I can come home once again and relate to those human beings who share with me the wonder and happiness and adversity and yes, triumph that are all part of the human condition. Fortunately, my instrument can change and transmit the music that those great geniuses before me have created and through the music, I can cause other people to share with me the emotion and experience that is life. It is through the playing of this instrument I can regain love lost and share with others the truth of life's realities and the inherent goodness of existence. These musical contexts that we are creating this very moment, can take others from the feelings of love to the depths of sorrow in a few well written sensitive passages, using the voices of the musicians' instruments, to take us through the journey of our own life experiences; an experience that lets us see the world through the eyes of a gifted composer who helps us to feel the emotional spectrum we may never encounter in any other way. Any art, including my art, is communication and we as humans desperately strive for communication; to make us feel that there is reason for living and that there are other humans that share our experiences and that we are basically the same, no matter what our lives have been before. My 'music of madness' is returning just to 'my music'. My music can now give us all a glimpse into the universality of our existence and let us feel pure emotion, untainted by our individual circumstances and embroidered from the material truth of our beings. Music by its very medium lets us touch real beauty and sense the truth as no other form of communication can. Great composers give us a chance to feel the joy of triumph, even if we have never experienced triumph before. Music lets us feel pure love, even if our lives have never been touched by the pure love of another.

As I listen to the quintet sending musical messages to the audience, it feels like the rebirth of my soul. It makes me feel the full range of my emotions without the dulling effects of the voice that has tortured my mind. I have returned at last to my true home. I listen intently, absorbing both the notes and the emotion and I feel as though the lover's kiss I had once anticipated, returns to greet me once more, as I move through this superb musical experience. The timbre of my flute cuts through the supporting harmonies created by my fellow quintet members and floats above it all, tethered lightly to the other instruments by a slim string of harmonies and the feelings in my heart. I am lost in the joy of creating the music I was born to perform; of singing out the emotions of the music's content. All five of us play the melody in unison, triumphant in our expression of this work's passionate message. My mind is filled with nothing but this music, its color, its truth, and its message of love which spreads along the very winds of reality. Even though that voice may still exist in my mind, I feel purified and strengthened in the knowledge that I have come home to my music at last, and I will triumph over the madness that had invaded its content for so many years. I am ready to regain my concert career and my life.

This is the musician's music, this is the musician's message to his audience, this is what life was meant to hold in its bosom as the reward for the struggles and the adversity; this is the meaning of my existence. We are as one entity feeling together, generating sound together, and stating our triumph together. The emotion of this moment touches the soul of all those that hear the exquisite sound. Together, if we are fortunate, for a few precious minutes we enable other human beings to see Faure's vision through our eyes thus bringing us together to feel the sameness of human experience, breaking through the loneliness of our human individuality. Such is the nature of all music, such is the nature of my music, and such is the nature of my life.

7

A Sweet Series of Encores

Winning the War

That first quintet rehearsal brought me fully back to the music that I love and I look forward anxiously to a performance before a live audience. I had chosen a small local theatre, and even without much publicity, we were able to fill the seats with former fans and friends of the musicians in the quintet. As we began to play Haydn that night, I once again felt the return of those wonderful emotions that can only be transmitted to the audience through music. I lost myself once again within the intricacies of Haydn's vision and before I realized it, our quintet were standing together and bowing to a grateful audience. I left the theatre that night confident once again that I could perform as a soloist on the concert stage.

The next morning, almost before I was fully awake, my mother popped her head in the door of my bedroom and said, "Dr. Sanduval is calling, Tracy. He says he wants to talk to you. Are you awake enough to take the call?" I respond, "You mean Maestro Sanduval?" My mother nods her head and with a slight grin on her face points to the phone and shuts my door. I answer the phone somewhat hesitatingly and hear the familiar timbre of the Maestro's best concert baritone asking me how I am. I hesitate for a moment, realizing that he probably knows of my visit to the Vistas of Heaven. I summon up my best professional voice and say, "I'm really fine (trying to put my best face on a difficult subject), "Oh, that's good" he replies, "I hope I did not wake you up?" "No", I answer trying to hide the fatigue in my voice—*, "I always get up early and begin practicing my flute as I watch the sunrise". (lie, lie). "Oh" he says, after a brief pause, "I had heard that you had had a brief illness. Are you feeling better now?" "Yes, thank you for asking. I have been quite ill, but I feel much better now and I've been doing some physical therapy as well as playing a few selected recitals." (This conversation was clearly aimed at finding out my true condition. The maestro may have heard of my visit to the Vistas of Heaven. He had certainly heard the playing of the crazy cadenza in that fateful earlier rehearsal). He questions me once again, but with a much more serious tone, "I was quite concerned Tracy after our last rehearsal when you left the hall without saying a word to me. And for all I knew you had either left the country or gone into seclusion, because I could not find anyone who could tell me what you were doing or where you were." Before I answer, I think silently to myself about the impact of what I might say and respond carefully to this great conductor who is so important to my future at this point in my career. I answer apologetically, "I realize that I left you rather hastily but I felt I had no choice at that time. I realize that what I did was unprofessional and I apologize deeply for what I did to you. I was extremely ill and needed to withdraw from my performance life in order to rest and regain my strength." There is a brief silence and I wait for the inevitable question from the maestro. "What was the nature of your illness? You must realize," he continues, "Your behavior that night did not appear to be normal. I was very concerned about your behavior and I am concerned that it might happen again. I love you as a flutist, you know that, but it concerns me when you appear to be hiding the truth about that last rehearsal."

I reply, "It's quite complicated, and yes, you deserve a more complete answer. Someday, we will sit down and I will tell you the full story. But for now, please just trust me. I am much better and I am prepared to play again, and above all I will not let you down. I can tell you, sincerely, that I love playing under your baton and appreciate deeply the great creativity you lend to any concert. I would love to play for you again, whether it's a minor piece or a major concerto."

The maestro's voice lightens a bit as he says, "I'm glad to hear that you are better, I accept your word as a professional, and I won't ask you, for now, about your illness. I hope it was not too serious. I am looking for someone once again to play the Nielsen Concerto and I feel you would be the perfect flutist to help me bring this great piece to life." After a brief pause, the maestro speaks again. "Would you consider giving it a second try?" I respond excitedly to this grand offer, "Maestro, it would be my honor to play with you once again. I will not let you down. I feel stronger than I ever have and you will be glad to hear that my flute is my full partner once again. As soon as you are ready, I will be there, just name the place and the time." The maestro responds quickly, "Good, I was hoping you would have that response and I have already placed the Nielsen on this season's program as the first piece." My only thoughts now were when the rehearsals would begin. After receiving a rehearsal schedule, I said my goodbyes to the maestro and began planning for my return to the stage I had once left in desperate pain.

I hung up the phone and ran into the kitchen to tell my mother the good news. She hugged me and smiled and said quietly, "I knew you would be ready. I have always known you would have the courage to return to the concert work you love." Then she gave me a very warm and fulfilling embrace and we walked out into the garden together to talk over the many plans that needed to be made before this performance could occur.

I had only three weeks to prepare for my return to the concert stage, but fortunately in the many months since leaving the hospital, I had been carefully preparing myself once again for the rigors of performance. I was ready for the performance of my life and the last final grand battle with the demons of my mind.

There were so many things to do before any normal major concert performance that I had little time to consider the return of that voice which helped destroy my career before. My mind was filled with practice sessions, selecting clothes, and the many other things that needed completion in preparation for my return to the concert stage. This concert would be my ultimate proving ground. I decided to approach the concerto with a fresh viewpoint. I threw out the old score, knowing it was still usable but I wanted to have a completely fresh start. This tattered and well-used score contained too many memories which I hoped to remove from my mind. This old score was a symbol of a difficult time in my life and a temporary ending to my musical career. Throwing out that score with its worn out cover and pencil-marked pages, symbolized the destruction of the angry voice of the soprano and that crazy cadenza and the desperate trip home from that last failed concert. Ridding myself of that old score would not cure my mind's shadowed problems, but it was my tearful reach for some reality within which I could live out my life. That old score represented to me, the now wrinkled and crumpled face of my former reality. It represented the aged view of that vicious soprano who had caused me endless pain and that last devastating rehearsal of Nielsen and of all the music that I loved. With a flourish, marking what I hoped would be the end of a long struggle, I literally opened a new page of my life and found within its freshness the unmistakable smell of fresh ink and the renewed vision of Nielsen and my musical life to come.

Now, I busied myself with many needed tasks that required completion, before I could pronounce myself ready to perform once again in that great concert hall within which I had left my tortured soul and an unfinished life. These tasks would take me many days and along with much rehearsing I soon readied myself for the dress rehearsal.

On the day of the dress rehearsal, I stared at my new dress with its own look of readiness for its place in this great performance. For a moment I held it up to my shoulders and looked in the mirror. I could see, in my mind, the far walls of the concert hall, behind my image, appearing in the distance and I imagined the lights dimming as I would raise my flute to an anxious audience, waiting to share with me the experience of hearing Nielsen's great music. I stood in this wishful reverie for a few moments and then heard the voice of my mother calling from the kitchen, "Better come in and get a quick bite to eat before you leave. You've only got an hour to get to the rehearsal." I smiled a slight knowing smile to myself. Just hearing those words, as mundane as they were, filled my life with the comfort and safety of belonging to a caring family. A family that had helped bring me from the depths of hell back to sanity; leaving unanswered their questions about my trips to strange places, filled with horrors they would never have to share, except through my eyes. Yet still wanting me to be part of that magical family "quintet" which helped fulfill my life and gave me the comfort and safety I needed. I answered quickly, "I'm coming mom, I'll be right there," and my mind quickly moved on to the battle ahead. The confrontation I knew was to come required strength. I hoped I would have the courage to play out this rehearsal in spite of the angry soprano, and to take one step closer to freedom from my illness.

I interrupted my final preparations for this evening's rehearsal and walked quickly to the dinner table. Dinner consisted of a brief snack. My mother knew that before any performance and especially this dress rehearsal, I would have the anxiety that comes with performing. More importantly, she also understood that my personal battle with my illness was about to take center stage. She gently put her hands around my shoulders as I are and whispered quietly in my ear, "Good luck on tonight's rehearsal, my heart is with you as always." and kissed me gently on the forehead. I reached my hand up towards her head and gave her a hug, letting her know I understood the depth of the unspoken message. I left the table and prepared quickly for the dress rehearsal playing a few quick excerpts, which included the more difficult passages of the Nielsen concerto. As I walked towards the door I stopped briefly to grab my musical paraphernalia plus my flute and my coat. I rushed quickly to the car and began the journey to the concert hall where Maestro Sandoval would be waiting for me, possibly along with the angry soprano. This drive was very different from the drive I had after the performance of that crazy cadenza. This time I felt confident that I would not be the one to leave the hall. I felt the determination that only the seasoned soldier can feel. I was not sure of the strategy I would use tonight, to overcome the angry soprano, but I had my mental armor in place and for a brief moment, felt the peace that comes with the experience of winning the day.

As I walk from my car to the theater, I feel an increasing sense of apprehension. I think silently to myself, "Maybe it's the stress of long hours of practice. Maybe it's the medication. Maybe it's just the result of voices too long lived with and the concern of too many battles lost." I stand for a moment in front of this theater that has been both a friend and an enemy. It seems like only yesterday that the stage within this theatre was witness to my ultimate professional disintegration. I feel my heart beating slightly faster and I realize that without my knowing it my body is preparing for the confrontation of my life. That bizarre cadenza fills my mind once again, and the horror of those moments, when I was near the full depth of my madness, regenerates within my body the fear that I felt and the helplessness of that moment. My body shivers with the remembrance of that moment when the angry soprano had done her best and brought me to my knees. My body stiffens and I wrap my arms around myself in an attempt to shake off these disturbing memories, and gathering all of my strength, I open the stage door of the theatre.

Once inside, I hear the familiar sounds of violins, violas, cellos and bass strings being patiently tuned and I listen to their mixed voices cascading across the empty theater creating an odd mixture of reverberations. Cutting through the thick sounds of strings being stretched and re–stretched are the winds playing quick liquid scales and through it all an incongruous accompaniment provided by the brass players who are practicing some of the more difficult excerpts from the concerto we are about to rehearse. These familiar sounds seem warm and act as friends to assure me that I am home with my music once again. I look for the maestro but he has yet to make an appearance. I feel breathless as I make my way backstage. John, the stagehand directs me to a small dressing room where I can warm up. John is in his late fifties and becomes excited about the trappings of the large concert as though he were a guest to the hall rather than its caretaker. As we approach the room, he begins to ask me something, but before he is even finished with the question, I hurriedly shut the door. I need to be alone to gather my thoughts; to calm down. The thick walls of the room keep the many noises of the theater out, creating a sound proof box. I can no longer hear the orchestra warming up, only the soft ticking of an old clock hanging on the wall. I quickly place my flute bag on an old table, with a small mirror on one end. In the silence of this small dressing room I turn all of my senses inward. I look again at the soft glow of the light as I assemble my flute and place it to my lips. I glance just briefly at the wall and the dark shadow of myself with the flute in place and I remember with bitterness the emptiness I felt at that moment two years ago when I wished that I was the shadow and could obtain the silent peace of its serene countenance. I begin to shiver. I don't think it's too cold. I place a wrap around my shoulders, but I continue to shiver. I know I should be warming up now with long tones, but I cannot stay inside this room alone any longer. Somehow even though music awaits me outside this door, I feel as though I am back in the quiet room of The Vistas and I know I have to run. I have to get out of this room. I open the door briskly and almost physically run into John the stagehand. He was about to knock on my door and give me the ten–minute call. I stop briefly to talk with John. He leans casually against the brick wall of the backstage area next to my dressing room. I look to my right and see the bright lights of the stage in the distance and I can hear the musicians continuing to warm up. "So how's it going this evening?" John asks in a very happy tone. "Do you feel alright? I had heard that you were sick." I look briefly back at the orchestra to my right before I answer, not being sure of the intent of his question. I Reply, "Oh yes, I feel much better now, thank you for asking." John nods and answers, "That's good, that's good." As he answers he nods his head up and down briefly, agreeing with himself, as though thinking thoughts that he does not share. Sometimes he acts as though he is having his own personal conversation and answering silently within his own mind. I am very familiar with that type of conversation. I've spent my own moments alone with my own voices for all too long. John continues to smile and nod his head up and down as I begin to hear a voice of my own, which I was praying would not come back this evening. This voice I know so well, begins to taunt me and even though her insults sting more than usual, I smile weakly again at John and ask him how he is doing. As he begins to answer, his voice begins to take on the hollowness of an echo and right there, just outside my dressing room, his body fades into nothingness and I see only the bare bricks and hear only the taunts of the voice inside my head. The grip on my flute tightens without my thinking about it. I begin to sweat imperceptibly. The medicine has to work. The medicine does work. I have been able to fight this before and I know I can. As I begin to walk slowly towards the lights of the stage, I try to think only of the cool feeling of the flute in my hands and the beautiful sounds of Nielsen that I will soon create this evening.

The steps to my place in front of the orchestra seem to come in slow motion. As I look towards the conductor, he sees my entrance and waves me towards him. He motions me to speak briefly with him. I am petrified but I try not to show it. I lean over to listen as he whispers something in my ear, "Good luck" he says quietly, his lips almost touching my ear as he speaks, "We are ready and I know you are ready. I know you won't let anything stop you this time." I take my place. The conductor cues the orchestra and we begin. Everything is as it should be except for that voice that is still there. I ignore her and try to focus on the first few phrases of the music. Once I begin playing, I feel a sense of comfort, but the voice continues. However, I am able to ignore her protestations. I continue to play and to feel the music. My body is now responding, as it should, to the true emotion of the sounds I am generating and not to the voice within my head. I feel emboldened; maybe it is the medications circulating through my brain. Maybe these medications have produced the shield that I need to continue this battle without failing. As the music moves inexorably towards my cadenza, I begin to feel the fear of a battle not yet won. I hold the A-flat that comes right before the cadenza. The soprano in my head is using every weapon she has to force me to play the cadenza in some distorted fashion as she had once before. As I try to ignore her, she becomes even louder, but when the moment comes for me to begin the cadenza I start to play it smoothly and beautifully as Nielsen created it. My fingers begin to fly over the notes in the cadenza and in spite of the voice inside me I continue to play this beautiful section as it was meant to be played. I silently applaud myself. I have won. The conductor looks at me and smiles and we continue the Nielsen uninterrupted. The music flows over the pain I have felt and my soul sings with the beauty of this great creation. As soon as the last notes sound through the empty hall, I begin to hear the muffled tapping of bows against music stands and the stamping of feet by the other musicians, saying wordlessly to me, your performance was great, you have won. I walk briskly over to the conductor and shake his hand. He looks down at me and says softly, "Do this tomorrow and I will be your fan forever. Now go home and get a good night's rest." I turn to the orchestra, waive a parting goodbye and take a short, self-conscious bow, thanking them for their appreciation of my performance.

I gather my things as quickly as possible and leave the theater, but this time I leave in triumph and without any tears in my eyes, except tears of joy. Feeling only happiness, I get into my car and speed home. When I walk in the door, it is 11:30pm and I walk quietly, expecting everyone to already be asleep. As I reach the center of our living room, I hear someone move and suddenly all the lights go on and there is my family and streamers that my sister and sister-in-law had carefully taped to the ceiling, and a big cake on the coffee table that says, 'Congratulations, you did it.' As usual, I had been so involved in my own thoughts that I did not fully realize that my family had lived those anxious moments with me and was prepared to give me the kind of applause that comes only from those who love you closely and share your dreams as well as your painful failings. I look around at each of them and see the love in their eyes, which one only receives on rare occasions from those that share your life. I look at everyone and exclaim triumphantly "I did it, I know what you've all had on your minds. But I did it. You all helped me and my doctor helped me and my medications helped me, but you were the ones who never gave up hope and I love you all for it." And even though I am smiling, the tears begin to flow and I feel an emotional release that was long in its coming.

I will not soon forget that wonderful evening, having triumphed over the voice in my head, and enjoying the loving care with which my family had greeted my return. We sat around the coffee table and ate cake and talked about my future plans and some of their own hopes and dreams and life was good once more. I hugged everyone and thanked them for a wonderful party and excused myself as I needed a good night's sleep before the performance.

I prepared myself for bed and because I was still somewhat excited over the evening's events I did not immediately fall asleep, but eventually my eyes closed and I began to dream. I remember the dream vividly, as it involved many of my mind's dark adventures. I felt it was my mind's final preparation for the last great struggle to regain my life and my career.

The dream begins in a great concert hall, the one in which I had practiced and performed the dress rehearsal for the Nielsen. But, as with all dreams, it has somehow changed. As with all great halls, it has a long reverberation time, but now the sounds bounce back and forth from the walls, playing against themselves without a reduction in amplitude until there is a mixture of music that can only be described as the descendent of the original tones coming from the orchestra. Strangely, although every orchestra instrument seems to be playing, I can only see empty orchestra chairs. The conductor is at the podium as he should be, but his feet somehow do not touch the podium, but rather float just above its level surface. The room is filled with smoke, or perhaps the fog of the subconscious, but its appearance is that of a heavy haze, possibly created by smokers in the audience. But in fact I can see no one in the audience. The chairs appear to be empty, although I can still hear a stray cough and people moving in their seats. As hard as I peer into that smoke–filled darkness, I can see no one. I wonder why I am performing the Nielsen without an audience, but in spite of this thought I bow to the audience in the hall, who I cannot see and I hear a loud echo of applause; not the applause itself, but a loud echo of the applause. That does not seem to bother me either and I nod to the conductor that I am prepared to play. The conductor raises his baton to the empty orchestra chairs and the music of Nielsen begins. My flute feels strangely heavy in my hands, but I try not to think about that as I begin to play my first entrance. Just lifting my flute to my lips requires all the strength in my arms. As I play, I began to hear that terrifying voice again, but this time it grows louder and louder. It is the angry soprano sharing this concert with me. She begins speaking to me, "You're playing is abominable. I don't know how the audience can stand it. You've had enough chances to quit. Why don't you just give up? You keep talking about battles but you don't win, you never win. Give me the damn flute and I'll show you how to play it." I feel a strange arm grab at me, and I step back and all the while the conductor is continuing to conduct and the orchestra members whom I cannot see, continue to play as though unaware of the horrendous battle that is beginning to take place. I look past the arm that has grabbed at me and move my head upward to stare at the person's face. It is the angry soprano. Even through the haze of the stage I somehow recognize her face. She has escaped the bounds of my mind and stands before me, ready to take away my music. Ready to take away my career. Ready to take away my soul. I cannot see her features clearly as the smoke swirls around her face. She is about my height and I find myself staring directly into her eyes as the orchestra continues to play. The smoke seems to dissipate with the passage of each bar. The last wisps of smoke are blown away from her face and I can now see her features clearly. Just at that moment, she grabs the flute from my hand and speaks, "The cadenza is coming up and I will play it—far better than you ever could." As she raises the flute to her mouth, I recognize in that instant, my own face on her distorted body. In this moment I have the revelation one can only have in a dream state. The soprano I hate so much is me. This voice I am fighting is my own voice. Those hands that control my fingers, forcing them to play that distorted cadenza are my own hands. And in that moment I realize that I am the one in control, not the voice. That I can change my life. That I can destroy this voice that has driven me to consider death. I rip the flute out of her hands and her mouth falls open wordlessly. She begins to look older and weaker. I grab her by the shoulders and throw her from the stage into the darkness of the audience. I hear one last echo of applause for that act and then I awake.

I sit upright in my bed and look at my clock. It's 4:15 am. I have hours to sleep and a lifetime to regain the joy of living I once knew. I realize as I turn over in bed and close my eyes, still remembering this dream, that I have met my enemy and it is me. I fall asleep quickly and without dreaming, I achieve the peaceful sleep of the redeemed.

Morning comes quickly and I feel strong and even more sure that my recovery will continue after having that fateful epiphany during the night. I feel ready for tonight's performance, but will I find the soprano waiting for me on stage? My mind races as I prepare to perform once more. The day race by as I am filled with joyous anticipation.

Later that evening as I walk on stage for my performance of Nielsen's Flute Concerto I realize that I am now truly ready to perform. It is time to step out from the lonely blackness of the shadows backstage and onto the exhilarating stage of life. Applause erupts as I walk confidently to center stage in my blue concert gown, but this time I can see the audience and hear more than the mere echo of their greeting. With that sound, I know that I am taking a major step towards recovering the consonant rich harmony of my mind that has been taken away from me for so long by my illness. I hesitate for an instant, standing in front of the orchestra. Thinking that I hear the dreaded sound of the soprano, I quickly turn my head towards the conductor and nod my readiness, knowing that the voice is really not present. There is only silence, thank God. The Maestro smiles at me as I ask for an "A" from the oboe. The principal oboe plays a pure "440 A". The silence in the theater, the audience there, waiting quietly, seems like an old friend, smiling from a distance. I adjust my flute, quietly checking and double–checking my intonation. I nod once more at the conductor and we begin the notes of the Nielsen.

As I play the last note of the last movement, I can hear the reverberations of this grand music against the walls of the huge hall and as the last note fades away, I hear the welcome applause of an appreciative audience. The angry soprano never made a single appearance during the entire performance. I have won. I know the war may not be over but I have confronted that terrible voice and those images that have disrupted my life for so long. I know they may not be silent forever, but now I can control them and begin to live once more that exuberant life that I once felt as I looked up from my grassy front lawn to see the blue mountains in the distance.

I lift my head high as the house lights come on in the theater and there in the front row I can see the faces of those people who have shared a bit of my life. The love I have given them through my music glows in their faces. I look for a brief moment past the audience's heads towards the back of the hall and I see in my mind's eye the silent figure of my grandfather, looking young and strong once more, as when we stood in front of the bright redness of his pomegranate tree; welcoming me back to the life I had once known.

Epilogue: A Complete Individual Despite a Brain Disorder

Throughout my illness I often asked myself, what is this thing we call life? I have spent a good portion of my life trying to find some clearer understanding of what life is all about; is it the same for each of us? Are there truths that we can find in some common reality, which allows us to share this experience we call existence? We are all in search of the truth in order to feel less alone.

Unfortunately, Schizoaffective disorder mercilessly skewed my view of reality and therefore robbed me, temporarily, of truly shared common experiences. I have found that it is through discovering this common reality that humans are privileged to experience, that we can become less alone. We do this through the myriad of ways that human beings can interact; through friendship, through love, through communication–reaching for that special connection that says to us that this is, at least, some of our common truth; this is a glimpse of the reality that we all share and therefore we are not alone.

I have been fortunate to share many new and wonderful truths with my family and colleagues since walking out of the shadows backstage. Since that triumphant moment when I returned to the concert stage, my life has been a series of new and wonderful adventures, unimpeded by the severe and unrelenting symptoms of my mental illness. The black depression no longer controls my life and my mind is no longer held prisoner by the angry soprano. There were three very important elements that made my recovery possible; the conscientious use of the antipsychotic medication *ZYPREXA®[1] as part of my drug therapy and the continuing support of my family and my personal physician. Thanks to these combined elements I have been able to perform on the concert stage once again.

I have continued to look for the challenges of a full life by trying my hand at music directorship of a church and also a symphony orchestra. I presently have a very rewarding research position with the Pacific Center for Advanced Studies where I help musicians who are preparing for the rigors of concert life. I now lecture as often as possible about my life, combining my music with the story of my recovery and passing on the message that there is hope for all of us with a mental illness.

I feel very fortunate to be able to live, work and have a successful life because of modern medicine and every day I am rediscovering connections between myself and the world around me, which allows me to enjoy shared experiences with family and friends once again.

Living with a mental illness is never easy, but it can be done, so just take a deep breath and walk into the spotlight with your head held high. Life is one beautiful concert that no one should miss, so persevere as I did, a sweet series of encores awaits you too.

---

1. *ZYPREXA® is a registered trademark of Eli Lilly and Company.

0-595-21256-5

Printed in the United States
6849